Devotions for a
Woman's Heart & Mind

Transformed

Published by Barbour Books, an imprint of Barbour Publishing, Inc., 1810 Barbour Drive, Uhrichsville, Ohio 44683, www.barbourbooks.com

Our mission is to inspire the world with the life-changing message of the Bible.

Member of the
Evangelical Christian
Publishers Association

Printed in China.

Devotions for a
Woman's Heart & Mind

Transformed

DONNA K. MALTESE

BARBOUR BOOKS
An Imprint of Barbour Publishing, Inc.

Introduction

*Let God transform you into a new person by changing the
way you think. Then you will learn to know God's will
for you, which is good and pleasing and perfect.*
ROMANS 12:2 NLT

Every moment of every day, thoughts are going through our minds, whether
we're conscious of them or not. Yet if we would stop our meanderings
and home in on what we're saying to ourselves, we might find many of
our thoughts are leading us to places where we (and God) would rather
not go. For *our thoughts are not God's thoughts* (Isaiah 55:8-9). But then
once we learn how to *become* more aware, more cognizant of what we're
thinking, we must also have the resources, tools, and weapons we need to
get our minds aligned with God's so that we can avoid the pitfalls of the

negative thoughts that lead to negative emotions, attitudes, dispositions, outlooks, and so much more.

Psychologist William James wrote, "The greatest weapon against stress is our ability to choose one thought over another." We can take that several steps further and say that choosing to be ruled by God's thoughts rather than our own will not only arm us against stress but all other negative forces that come against us, ones that keep us from doing and being what God would have us do and be.

Within these pages, you'll find a method to "destroy arguments and every lofty opinion raised against the knowledge of God, and take every thought captive to obey Christ" (2 Corinthians 10:5 ESV). A guide to aid you as you build your life, faith, and thoughts on the rock-solid foundation of Christ (see Matthew 7:24-29; Luke 6:47-49). A resource to help you exchange your fear-laden worries with God's comforting words that will cheer and delight your soul (Psalm 94:18-19 AMPC). A handbook to help you learn to walk in "the unforced rhythms of grace" (Matthew 11:29 MSG) with Jesus. A pathway to the peace of God's wisdom, truth, and knowledge (see Philippians 4:4-9).

As you work your way through the pages that follow and begin to renew your mind at every juncture (see Romans 12:1-2), changing up your thoughts to be more like God's, you'll find yourself singing a new song (see Psalm 96:1). You'll be living a life where your thoughts have become agreeable to God's. You'll be seeing your plans succeed, and your words, actions, and attitude transforming your world.

Roll your works upon the Lord [commit and trust them wholly to Him; He will cause your thoughts to become agreeable to His will, and] so shall your plans be established and succeed.

PROVERBS 16:3 AMPC

How to Use This Book

*"These words I speak to you are not incidental additions
to your life, homeowner improvements to your standard
of living. They are foundational words, words to build a life
on. If you work these words into your life, you are like a
smart carpenter who built his house on solid rock."*

MATTHEW 7:24 MSG

Welcome to *Transformed: Devotions for a Woman's Heart and Mind*, a book that can be used to change your heart, mind, and life. For God wants us to not just hear His words and promises but to act upon them and live them out. Not just to read Jesus' teachings and ideas but to take His thoughts in and make them ours, to build our faith upon them, to use them as foundation principles for our lives. For "Unless the LORD builds the house, those who build it labor in vain" (Psalm 127:1 ESV).

Our lives need to be built upon God's Word so that we'll not be tossed by the wind and waves (Ephesians 4:11-15). This all really comes down to your thinking. Are your thoughts made up of your sand or Jesus' rock? Jesus, of course, wants your life, your thoughts, the foundation of your faith to be built on the solid rock of His Word. For He knows that as you think in your heart, so you will be (Proverbs 23:7 KJV).

Thus, *Transformed: Devotions for a Woman's Heart and Mind* has been written to get you, your faith, and your thoughts off the sinking sand and onto the rock-solid foundation of God's Word. To help you get there from here, each reading begins with Bible verses from both the Old and the New Testaments, each one supporting or expanding on the other, demonstrating that God has wanted His people to have this rock-solid foundation of thought since the very beginning of time.

Following the verses from God's Word are readings that will explore a negative thought that may be ruling your life, holding you back from being all God has designed you to be. You will discover how that particular thought is a lie because it goes against the truth and proof of God's Word.

After the reading is a prayer asking God to help you turn your mind and life around, helping you let go of the negative thought and replace it with one that will transform your mind, heart, and life. Finally, at the bottom of the page is a thought you can use for the hours, days, weeks, months, or years that follow, a thought that will replace the lie with God's truth.

Please take your time as you go through these readings. Doing so will better ensure that the new thoughts stick in your heart and mind so that when you need to pull from God's well of truths, you will find a fountain of wisdom already instilled within you.

Yet there may be times when you find you need immediate guidance and power to help you shore up your faith. For those moments, go to the index at the back of the book. There you will find a list of emotions, feelings, and mind-sets that will guide you to the remedy you need within God's precious Word for you, for life.

May you be blessed as you take this transformational journey deep into God's territory of truth, love, and provision. May your daily prayer be. . .

O God, stay with me; let no word cross my lips that is not your word, no thoughts enter my mind that are not your thoughts, no deed ever be done or entertained by me that is not your deed.
MALCOLM MUGGERIDGE

As the Spirit Moves

The good person is generous. . .a. . .lasting reputation.
Unfazed by rumor and gossip, heart ready, trusting in GOD,
Spirit firm, unperturbed, ever blessed. . . . "She did what she could
when she could. . . . And you can be sure that. . .what she
just did is going to be talked about admiringly."

PSALM 112:5-8; MARK 14:8 MSG

As Jesus sat at a table in Simon the leper's home, a woman approached Him. In her hand was an expensive alabaster bottle. Within it was a very costly perfume valued at more than 300 denarii, the equivalent of a common laborer's annual income. "Opening the bottle, she poured it on his head" (Mark 14:3 MSG).

Jesus' disciples protested! They considered the perfume as wasted—on Jesus! They argued that the flask and its contents could have been sold and given to the poor. So they "swelled up in anger, nearly bursting with indignation" (Mark 14:5 MSG).

Jesus spoke up for this unnamed woman, telling His followers to leave her alone. For she'd followed the promptings of the Spirit. Showing a sincere dedication to and love for Jesus, she went against the norm. She, a lone woman in a male-dominated society, put her Savior above all else—money, position, and human reasoning.

When you feel as if you are powerless to do anything with what you have to offer, you may begin thinking you're too tiny a cog in the wheel

of life to be of any effect. That what you do means nothing.

Yet Jesus would have you think otherwise. He sees all that you're doing and commends your efforts. He values those who follow the promptings of God, not man. He sticks up for those who put Him, His Father, and His Spirit before all else. He honors those who are humble, do their best, lovingly worship Him, give Him what they have—whether it be little or much—and leave the results of their efforts to Him.

Be as this woman (see Mark 14:3-9), open to the promptings of the Holy Spirit, doing what you can, when and where you can, with what you have. And Jesus will smile upon your efforts.

Lord, help me to do what I can with what I am and have.
To put You above all else—money, position, and human
reasoning. In this moment, I open myself to You,
following where the Spirit moves me.

I will do what I can for God, just as the Spirit moves me.

Found by a Mighty God

"I have called you by name, you are mine." . . .
*"The sheep hear [the Good Shepherd's] voice, and he calls
his own sheep by name and leads them out. . . . He goes
before them, and the sheep follow him, for they know
his voice. . . . I am the good shepherd."*
ISAIAH 43:1; JOHN 10:3-4, 11 ESV

It's easy to feel lost in this world. To feel nameless, unnoticed, neglected, overlooked. Yet the truth is that God is in your very midst. He's loved you like no other, even before you loved Him. In fact, He has called you by your very name. He—the King and Sustainer of the universe, the Master of creation—claims and names you as His own!

You are the daughter of God. He has singled you out, picked you from the crowd, chosen you from the flock. And because you are His very own and very precious lamb, He sent His Son, Jesus, not just to save you but to call you out, apart from all the rest!

Jesus is your Good Shepherd. He loves you so much that He laid His life down for you. As you drown out all the noise and distractions of this world, you can hear Him call you by name. And when you hear your name and follow that familiar voice, you'll know where to go. And if, by some chance, you do go astray, you know Jesus will come looking for you. He'll rescue you over and over again.

So, on those days when you're feeling lost, nameless, and neglected,

know that God has called you by name. He's keeping a sharp eye on you. He's chosen you, His precious daughter, to be reconciled with Him. And while you're here on earth, you can be sure Jesus is here for you, acting as your front guard and guide, doing anything and everything to keep you safe by His side. He'll shepherd you, lead you to green pastures where you can find nourishment for your soul and the peace of still waters.

Listen. He's calling your name.

Father God, thank You for naming me as Your own. And for sending Your Son, my Good Shepherd, to not just save me but to lead and guide me. Open my ears so that I can hear You calling my name! In Jesus' name I pray, amen.

I am not lost but found by a mighty God, who knows and calls me by name.

Supernatural Protection

He will order his angels to protect you wherever you go.
They will hold you up with their hands so you
won't even hurt your foot on a stone. . . .
Peter finally came to his senses. "It's really true!"
he said. "The Lord has sent his angel and saved me!"
PSALM 91:11-12; ACTS 12:11 NLT

This world can be a scary place, as the daily news and ads for the latest home-security system keep reminding you. Even children are taught about stranger danger. All this may leave you alarmed, thinking you have no one to protect you, no one looking out for you, no one keeping watch over you.

Yet God would have you remember that "The angel of the Lord stays close around those who fear Him, and He takes them out of trouble" (Psalm 34:7 NLV). No human may have realized this truth more than the disciple Peter.

After King Herod killed James, the brother of John, he had Peter put in prison and bound in chains. As Peter fell asleep between two soldiers, an angel of the Lord came and stood beside him. A bright light shone in the cell. The angel shook Peter awake and told him to get up. That's when Peter's chains fell off. Then the angel told Peter to get dressed and follow him. As Peter did so, "He did not know that what was being done by the angel was real, but thought he was seeing a vision" (Acts 12:9 ESV).

They passed the first and second guards before coming to an iron gate that led into the city. The gate "opened for them of its own accord" (Acts 12:10 ESV)! And as they headed down one of the city streets, the angel left him. That's when Peter finally came to his senses. He knew he'd been rescued by an angel!

Although you may never experience an angel's rescue in such a dramatic fashion, know this: God *has* ordered His angels to keep an eye on you, to protect and defend you wherever you go. And to comfort and take care of you wherever you land, just as they did Jesus (Matthew 4:11).

Lord, thank You for taking such good care of me, for watching over me, and for ordering Your angels to help me in so many ways. Thanks for this reminder that with You in my life, I am never alone or left unprotected. For I am in Your tender care. Amen.

I need not fear, for I'm under the protection of God's angels.

More Than Good Enough

*The angel of the LORD appeared to [Gideon] and said,
"Mighty hero, the LORD is with you!" . . . "Simon. . .
my Father in heaven has revealed this to you. . . .
Now I say to you that you are Peter (which means
'rock'), and upon this rock I will build my church."*
JUDGES 6:12; MATTHEW 16:17-18 NLT

Some people are beyond proud. Others are beyond humble. They don't think they're good enough—for themselves, others, or God.

Gideon had that mind-set. When God's people were in trouble, an angel of the Lord came to him. The first words out of the angel's mouth were, "Mighty hero, the LORD is with you!" He then proceeded to tell Gideon that God was sending him to rescue Israel from her enemies, telling him to "Go with the strength you have" (Judges 6:14 NLT). Gideon couldn't believe his ears. His response was, "How can I rescue Israel? My clan is the weakest. . .and I am the least in my entire family!" (Judges 6:15 NLT). God's response was, "No worries. I'll be with you every step of the way." And God was true to His word. He stuck by Gideon, enabling him to rescue God's people.

Thousands of years later, Jesus told Simon his new name would be Peter and that He would build His church upon him. This disciple would later deny Jesus not once but three times! Yet, after Jesus' resurrection and ascension, Peter became a strong Christian, playing an essential

role in establishing God's church!

The point is that God already sees you as the person more than good enough, more than capable of doing what He has called you to do. Change your perspective of yourself to His. See yourself as someone whom God has made and will continue to make more than good enough. As someone He's building up to be a mighty heroine, to help lift and rescue others. To be someone on whom He can build a body of believers.

Simply believe God is with you—because He is. Go in the strength you have, knowing you're more than good enough. After all, you are the daughter of a King and the sister of a Prince.

Thank You, Lord, for being with me. For giving me all the strength I need to do what You've called me to do—and so much more. In You I believe. In Jesus' name I pray, amen.

I'm more than able to do what God has called me to do.

Restored with Hope

*David was greatly distressed. . . . But David
encouraged and strengthened himself in the Lord. . . .
Father, if You are willing, remove this cup from Me; yet not
My will, but [always] Yours be done. And there appeared to
Him an angel from heaven, strengthening Him in spirit.*

1 SAMUEL 30:6; LUKE 22:42-43 AMPC

At times, things may seem hopeless. Mired in grief, unsure of the future, or too weak to continue on, where does one go? To God.

David and his men had just returned home when they found their village burned down and their families taken captive. David and his men "wept until they had no more strength to weep" (1 Samuel 30:4 AMPC). Not only was David devastated but his "men spoke of stoning him because the souls of them all were bitterly grieved" (1 Samuel 30:6 AMPC). Where could he turn? To God. There David regained not only his courage and strength but his hope and direction, allowing him to not only win back what he'd lost but acquire even more!

Jesus, fully God and human, knew His torture and death would soon come. Agonized over the future, He went to Father God, dropped to His knees, and prayed. From God, Jesus received the spiritual hope, courage, and strength He needed to meet His final challenge.

When you don't see a way out, when your mind tells you there's no hope, turn to God. Through your tears, agony, and heartache, pray. Plant

these words of truth in your heart: "I would have been without hope if I had not believed that I would see the loving-kindness of the Lord in the land of the living" (Psalm 27:13 NLV). Tell your soul, "Wait for the Lord. Be strong. Let your heart be strong" (Psalm 27:14 NLV).

As you do so, God will encourage you. He'll send His angels to give you all the strength you need. He'll fill you with hope, restoring what you've lost—and adding even more!

When I feel hopeless, Lord, turn me to You. Lift up my chin so that my gaze will turn upward to You. Give me the strength and courage that I need to face whatever happens. I believe I will see Your loving-kindness in this land of the living. Wait, my soul. Wait for God. Be strong. Yes, wait. God will restore you. Amen.

In God, I overflow with hope. From God, I regain strength and courage.

Forever Loved

"The LORD your God is living among you. He is a mighty
savior. He will take delight in you with gladness.
With his love, he will calm all your fears." . . .
"God so loved the world that He gave His only Son.
Whoever puts his trust in God's Son will not
be lost but will have life that lasts forever."
ZEPHANIAH 3:17 NLT; JOHN 3:16 NLV

Relationships can be very challenging. Those we cherish—mothers, fathers, sisters, brothers, partners, and friends—may desert or betray us. They may take us for granted, insult us, or neglect us. In these situations, we may begin thinking, *No one loves me.*

Relationships with people are like a roller-coaster ride. Some days you're riding high; other days you're dipping pretty low—and in both instances, you may be screaming in fear. In the movie *An Affair to Remember*, Debra Kerr's character asks, "What makes life so difficult?" Cary Grant's character, wincing, replies somewhat playfully yet honestly, "People?"

Although you may encounter people problems, you need never feel unloved. For there's a supernatural Someone who adores you like no other: God. He loves you so much He sent His Son, Jesus, to die for your sins. Through Jesus, you have been reconciled to God. You're precious in His sight, a recipient of His eternal love for which you can never be separated.

To help you grasp the intimacy of Jesus' adoration of you, imagine

Him, your Beloved, speaking to you, saying, "Rise up, my love, my fair one, and come away" (Song of Solomon 2:10 AMPC). Enter into His presence, lean back, lay your weary head down upon His chest. Say to yourself, "[I can feel] his left hand under my head and his right hand embraces me!" (Song of Solomon 2:6 AMPC).

In this moment, realize the truth. You are loved. You are worthy.

In the movie *Charade*, Cary Grant says to Audrey Hepburn, "You should see your face." She says, "What's the matter with it?" He says, "It's lovely." That's what your Beloved says to you.

Know that you are lovely, loved, and lovable. Never doubt it. Plant that truth in your mind. Lean back upon Jesus and feel Him, your Beloved, touch your heart. Bask in that intimate glow.

Dear Jesus, thank You for loving me in all my days and nights.
As I lean back upon You, pull me close. Never let me go.
In Your name I pray, amen.

I am drenched in the love of my Lord.

Stepping Out

Go for yourself [for your own advantage] away
from your country, from your relatives and your
father's house, to the land that I will show you. . . .
[Urged on] by faith Abraham, when he was called,
obeyed and went forth to a place which he was destined to
receive as an inheritance; and he went, although he did not
know or trouble his mind about where he was to go.
GENESIS 12:1; HEBREWS 11:8 AMPC

When you're not sure which direction to take, fear can set in. Afraid of moving forward, you have a pretty good chance of missing out on the opportunity God is waiting for you to take Him up on. So how do you get yourself moving? How do you get the courage to move out of your comfort zone?

You dig deep into your faith and God's Word. You look at the story and example of Abram. A seventy-five-year-old man, married yet childless. A man to whom God promised more descendants and blessings—for himself and those who blessed him—than he could count.

All these promises may seem unbelievable. But not to Abraham. For he had faith in God—to lead, advise, direct, and provide for him. That faith was what urged Abram to obey God. To go when and where he was called. Even though he didn't know where he was going.

Urged on by his faith, Abram stepped out, away from his country,

relatives, and friends. He turned his back on everyone and everything familiar to him. And he did so with no worries about what might lie ahead. There was no anxiety or angst about the fact that he had no idea the route of his journey. He did not "trouble his mind about where he was to go." Abram just left all the details up to God, knowing that He would take care of him every step of the way.

Today, allow your faith—"the assurance (the confirmation, the title deed) of the things [we] hope for, being the proof of things [we] do not see *and* the conviction of their reality [faith perceiving as real fact what is not revealed to the senses]" (Hebrews 11:1 AMPC)—to move you out of fear and into following.

Lord, even though I cannot see the future, I know You can.
I also know that as soon as I obey You, You will be here to lead,
advise, direct, and provide for me, every step of the way as
I step out in faith, in You. Amen.

My faith gives me the courage to move forward with God.

A New Focus

"God. . .we have no power against all these men who are coming against us. We do not know what to do. But our eyes look to You." . . .
"They were to look for God. Then they might feel after Him and find Him because He is not far from each one of us."
2 CHRONICLES 20:12; ACTS 17:27 NLV

When something big is coming against you, you may begin thinking, "There's no way I can handle this. There's nothing I can do." But there is!

Jehoshaphat, king of Judah, was in deep trouble. Three different enemy nations had formed an army that was set to attack him and his people. He knew his army could not defeat the enemy horde. Although full of fear, "Jehoshaphat. . .set himself [determinedly, as his vital need] to seek the Lord" (2 Chronicles 20:3 AMPC). He called his people to pray with him to God with all their hearts.

In his prayer, Jehoshaphat reminded God, himself, and the people that God held all the power. That in the past God had driven out the enemy. Then the king cried for help, knowing God would hear and save them, ending with, "We have no power to overcome our enemy. We have no clue what to do. But we're looking to You."

That's when God's Spirit spoke to the king, saying, "Do not be afraid or troubled. . . . For the battle is not yours but God's. . . . Just stand still in your places and see the saving power of the Lord work for you. . . . For the Lord is with you" (2 Chronicles 20:15, 17 NLV).

When you're faced by something you can't handle, pray. Tell God about your situation. He holds all the power. Remind Him (and yourself) of past situations in which He saved His people. Then ask for His help, knowing He'll hear you and save you. Tell Him you don't know what to do, but your eyes are on Him.

Then take to heart—and mind—His command not to be afraid. For this is His battle. Then stand still and let Him work.

Lord, I know that what I can't handle, You can! Today I take to heart—and mind—Your command that I need not be afraid but let You fight my battles. Here I stand, in Your peace, still and calm, allowing You to work. In Jesus' name I pray, amen.

I'm still and calm, knowing God can handle what I cannot.

Never Too Young

"Don't be ridiculous!" Saul replied. "There's no way you can
fight this Philistine and possibly win! You're only a boy." . . .
Don't let anyone think less of you because you are young.
Be an example to all believers in what you say, in the way
you live, in your love, your faith, and your purity.

1 SAMUEL 17:33; 1 TIMOTHY 4:12 NLT

Chances are, there was a time in your life when you wanted to do something. And after summoning up your courage to offer your services, someone says, "There's no way you can do this. You're just a girl!" If you hear that, or any other words of discouragement, often enough, you begin to think it's true. Next thing you know, you find yourself going through life afraid to try anything that even looks like a challenge.

When David was told he was too young to fight a full-grown giant, he didn't give up. Instead, "David persisted" (1 Samuel 17:34 NLT). He told the king he'd fought off both lions and bears when shepherding his flock. And just as he'd killed those predators, he'd kill Goliath. Yet—and this is the important part—he added that it was through the Lord that he'd won and would win again in the battle, saying, "The LORD who rescued me from the claws of the lion and the bear will rescue me from this Philistine!" (1 Samuel 17:37 NLT). Hearing that, Saul let David fight the Philistine and, of course, he won!

In his letter to Timothy, a young church leader, the apostle Paul backs

up the idea that age should not deter anyone from serving God. Paul encouraged Timothy to allow no one to give him a hard time because of his youth, and to be an example to others and use the gifts God gave him to serve.

This is good advice for you, no matter what your age. If God has called you to do something for Him, don't let how others view you stand in your way. Don't allow their discouraging and disparaging comments to keep you from using your gifts. Instead, persist in serving God, knowing He will give you the power to overcome.

Help me, Lord, to not let the criticisms of others get into my head, leading me to believe I'm not able to do what You have called me to do. Give me the confidence and right thinking I need to use the gifts You've given me. Amen.

I can successfully serve God no matter what my age.

Mission Possible

*O Sovereign LORD! You made the heavens and earth by your
strong hand and powerful arm. Nothing is too hard for you! . . .
Jesus looked at them intently and said, "Humanly speaking,
it is impossible. But with God everything is possible."*

JEREMIAH 32:17; MATTHEW 19:26 NLT

A task lies before you. Yet you hesitate to start. You doubt you have the energy, much less the know-how, to do what needs to be done. Or perhaps a problem arises, but you see no possible solution on the horizon. Or you find yourself in a predicament yet see no way out.

It's in those situations that the thought *"This is impossible"* can creep into your mind. It's a powerful and common lie that can easily make its way into your heart and cause you to throw up your arms in defeat before you even attempt to start the assignment, solve the problem, or find your way out of your difficulty. Yet the truth is that *nothing is impossible* if you go to God and ask Him for help.

It's true. It says so in God's Word! God says you can do all things through Christ who gives you strength (Philippians 4:13); that if you have faith the size of a mustard seed, you can move mountains (Matthew 17:20); that if you desire something, pray about it, and believe you'll get it, you will (Mark 11:24)!

You are the daughter of a King. The One who speaks things into being. The Lord God is the One who parts seas, makes the sun stand

still, and causes the earth to open up—all for the benefit of His faithful followers. His Son, Jesus, changes water into wine, raises people from the dead, and heals the sick.

So it's time to get it into your head and write it on your heart that nothing is impossible when you are with God and He is with you. There is nothing too hard for Him. That is the rock-solid truth that can transform your life.

All you have to do is put what seems like an impossibility before God. Then let it go. Know that God will do the work Himself or through you. The point is you need not worry about the task, problem, or predicament. Simply rest in God, knowing He can do anything beyond what you can think or imagine.

With You, Lord, anything is possible. Help me to write that truth upon my heart and mind. For I know that once I am confident of the fact that nothing is too hard for You, my life will be transformed. In Jesus' name I pray, amen.

With God in my life and heart, nothing is impossible!

Calm, Cool, and Collected

In returning [to Me] and resting [in Me] you shall be saved;
in quietness and in [trusting] confidence shall be your strength. . . .
Take My yoke upon you and learn of Me. . .and you will
find rest (relief and ease and refreshment and
recreation and blessed quiet) for your souls.
ISAIAH 30:15; MATTHEW 11:29 AMPC

Life is full of surprises. Just when you've settled into a routine, some unanticipated event occurs, stopping you in your tracks, turning your world on its head. Your thoughts run wild. Your heart begins to race as you try to figure out what to do, who to talk to, perhaps even where to hide.

Yet those are the exact moments when God would have you come to Him—and only Him. Speaking through Isaiah, God says you are to rest in Him. To put all your trust and confidence in Him. Millennia later, Jesus reinforces this idea, telling His followers that in Him they will find the rest they need to quiet and refresh their souls.

After Jesus was born, angels stopped some shepherds in their tracks. They told them a Savior had been born in a manger. When the shepherds traveled to Bethlehem, found Jesus, and told everyone what the angels had announced, their listeners were stunned. "But Mary was keeping within herself all these things (sayings), weighing *and* pondering them in her heart" (Luke 2:19 AMPC). She had the same response when years later she found the boy Jesus in the temple, His Father's house

(Luke 2:49), listening to and asking questions of religious scholars who were amazed at His knowledge. When the family got back home, Mary "kept *and* closely and persistently guarded all these things in her heart" (Luke 2:51 AMPC).

Make Mary your example. When you find yourself startled by life, stunned by events, not knowing what to think or do, go to God. Rest your head upon His shoulder. Calmly weigh and ponder things in your heart. Allow God to take your thoughts from racing to rest, to give you the confidence and strength you're craving. Only then will you begin thinking calmly and clearly and find your way forward.

Lord, I want to be calm, cool, and collected no matter what life brings my way. So I'm coming to You for the rest and relief I need. Quiet my racing thoughts. Refresh my soul and spirit as I lean back into You. In Jesus' name, amen.

My thoughts are calm as I rest in Jesus.

Guarded Peace

You will guard him and keep him in perfect and constant peace
whose mind. . .is stayed on You, because he commits himself
to You, leans on You, and hopes confidently in You. . . .
Then you will experience God's peace, which exceeds anything
we can understand. His peace will guard your hearts
and minds as you live in Christ Jesus.
ISAIAH 26:3 AMPC; PHILIPPIANS 4:7 NLT

This is a world full of noise, information, natural disasters, gun violence, discrimination, and various wars on nations, drugs, injustices, poverty, and more. Each day a new battle is brewing somewhere, in business, politics, work, and within families and churches. It's enough to make one despair of ever finding peace.

Yet God has told you that if you keep your mind on Him, He will not only guard you and your heart and mind, but He will also keep you in perfect and constant peace. That's all very well and good, but how do you get into that peace every day?

First you need to understand the peace promised. In this imperfect and stressful world, you'll continue to experience difficulties. But Jesus tells you, "take heart; I have overcome the world" (John 16:33 ESV). He wants you to be confident that He has the resurrection power to help you overcome all the challenges you face.

To get yourself out of your current chaos and into God's eternal

calm, you need to keep your mind "stayed on" Him. That means to fix your thoughts on Him. To train yourself to meditate on His presence and power. That involves opening up, feasting upon, and meditating on God's Word (Psalm 119:15). Memorizing the verses that really speak to your heart and mind. (Consider beginning with the soothing words of Isaiah 26:3.) Then trust God, committing yourself to Him, leaning on Him, and hoping confidently in Him (Isaiah 26:4).

Additional steps to perfect peace are outlined by Paul who writes, "Don't worry about anything; instead, pray about everything. Tell God what you need, and thank him for all he has done. Then you will experience God's peace" (Philippians 4:6-7 NLT).

Now that you have the tools to get to peace, it's up to you to implement them. Why not begin that journey today?

Prince of Peace, be with me on this journey into You. Help me obtain the perfect and constant peace You promise, the peace that surpasses all understanding. In Jesus' name, amen.

Focused on God, I am filled with perfect peace.

Never Alone

"I am with you, and I will protect you wherever you go. . . . I will not leave you until I have finished giving you everything I have promised you." Then Jacob awoke from his sleep and said, "Surely the LORD is in this place, and I wasn't even aware of it!" . . . [Jesus said] "Be sure of this: I am with you always."
GENESIS 28:15-16; MATTHEW 28:20 NLT

When the result of your misdeeds has you on the run, do you ever wonder where God is? Do you wonder if God has deserted you?

Consider Jacob. Prompted by his mother Rebekah, Jacob stole his older brother's blessing. Once he did so, he knew his life was in danger. So on the pretext of having to look for a suitable wife, Jacob ran away from home.

That first night Jacob stopped to rest. Using a stone for a pillow, he fell asleep and dreamed of angels going up and down a ladder reaching from heaven to earth. Standing above it, the Lord spoke, promising He'd always be with Jacob, never leaving him. When Jacob woke, he was stunned, for he realized that even in that place, God was with him.

When Jesus died on the cross, His followers felt alone and abandoned. How stunned they were when Jesus reappeared, resurrected from death, assuring His followers He'd always be with them.

The same holds true for you. No matter what you do, no matter where you go, no matter what you might be running from, don't despair

or think you've been abandoned. Because God is with you. Always. Even if you're not aware of it, He is by your side.

When you were in your mother's womb, God saw you. He knows when you stand up and sit down. God even knows what you're thinking! So plant this truth firmly in your mind: God is with you—loving, protecting, leading, guiding, and helping you—on every step of your journey through this life and beyond.

The fact that You, Lord, are always with me, no matter where I go, no matter what I've done, amazes me! Although others may desert me, You will always be here. Help me become more and more aware of Your presence in and with me. In Jesus' name, amen.

God is always by my side, helping, loving, leading.

Finding Favor

*Trust in the Lord with all your heart, and do not trust
in your own understanding. Agree with Him in all
your ways, and He will make your paths straight. . . .
"Do not let your heart be troubled. You have put
your trust in God, put your trust in Me also."*

PROVERBS 3:5-6; JOHN 14:1 NLV

Life can be complicated. Just when you think you've got everything figured out, you lose or gain a job, house, spouse, child, parent, friend, or pastor. Suddenly you're out of your comfort zone, trying desperately to figure out what to do, how to proceed. Confusion in your outer world stirs up confusion in your inner world.

Mary—a young virgin living in Nazareth and engaged to a man named Joseph—became confused when the angel Gabriel appeared out of nowhere and told her she'd been favored and chosen by God. This news left Mary "greatly troubled *and* disturbed *and* confused at what he said and kept revolving in her mind what such a greeting might mean" (Luke 1:29 AMPC).

Gabriel said, "Don't be afraid. Because God favors you, you're going to have His Son and call Him Jesus. He'll be the king forever!"

Mary says, "Okay. . .but how exactly is this going to happen?" The angel gives her the details, ending with, "God can do anything." And she responds with, "Let Him use me as He will."

Following God's will, the amazingly pliant Mary became pregnant. Unmarried, she bore the shame of those around her, people who didn't understand what God was doing. Yet still, she followed Him. How did she do it?

Mary lived by the precepts in Proverbs 3:1-6. She followed God's teachings, storing them in her heart, and, in so doing, found favor in the sight of God and man. She trusted her Lord with her entire being and life. What she didn't understand she left in His hands. As she lived this way, in God's will, He kept her on track.

You too can find God's favor, living and loving fully and well, by letting your confusion and troubles fall away as you put all Your trust in God and His Word, following His will and way. Ready? Set? Go!

I'm no longer going to try to figure out all You have planned for me, Lord. I'm just going to stay close to You, trust You, and follow You. In Jesus' name, amen!

God blesses my life as I put all my trust in His Word, will, and way.

Power Up

They who wait for the LORD shall renew their strength;
they shall mount up with wings like eagles; they shall
run and not be weary; they shall walk and not faint. . . .
If God is for us, who can be against us?
ISAIAH 40:31; ROMANS 8:31 ESV

What do you do when your fear-filled thoughts fill you with so much despair and discouragement that you feel you cannot go on?

On Mount Carmel Elijah literally had a mountaintop experience, successfully proving the superiority of God over the false idol Baal. Soon after, Queen Jezebel, a Baal enthusiast, threatened to kill Elijah. So he ran for his life into the wilderness. After a day's journey, he sat down and told God, "That's it. I'm done. Kill me now. I'm no better than my ancestors," then fell asleep.

An angel touched him, telling him to get up and eat. Seeing cake and some cool water, he ate, drank, and then fell back to sleep. The angel of God returned, touched him, and said, "Arise and eat, for the journey is too great for you" (1 Kings 19:7 ESV). So Elijah ate, then "went in the strength of that food forty days and forty nights to Horeb, the mount of God" (1 Kings 19:8 ESV).

It was there, in the quiet stillness, that God came to Elijah, asking, "What are you doing here?" Elijah related how much he'd done for God. That His people had abandoned Him. That he was the only prophet left,

and now someone was out to kill him. In a low whisper, God told Elijah to go back the way he came. To get back on *His* track.

Elijah had had so many successes when following God. He'd raised a child from the dead, called down the fire of God, and provided a poor widow with a miraculous supply of flour and oil. Yet in spite of all that, even he was brought down into despair by the threat of one woman.

When you find yourself so desperate and discouraged that you feel you cannot take one more step, don't run away. Go to God, the all-powerful and present God who is with you. He'll give you the rest, nourishment, encouragement, and strength you need to rise back up as you wait on Him.

Here I am, Lord. Please give me the rest, nourishment, strength, and encouragement I need to go on, to get back on Your track. Amen.

In God I have all the strength I need to go on.

Blessed in Believing

The Lord has done what He planned;
He has carried out and finished His word. . . .
Blessed (happy, to be envied) is she who believed
that there would be a fulfillment of the things
that were spoken to her from the Lord.
LAMENTATIONS 2:17; LUKE 1:45 AMPC

Has God ever promised you something so extraordinary that you weren't certain He could or would really keep His word?

The priest Zachariah and his wife, Elizabeth, were right with God, obedient to Him in every way. Yet they had no children and were both quite elderly. One day while Zachariah was on temple duty, the angel Gabriel told the priest his prayer had been heard. He proclaimed that Elizabeth would have a son, John, who would do great things for God.

Zachariah couldn't wrap his head around this news, so he said, "Do you expect me to believe this? I'm an old man and my wife is an old woman" (Luke 1:18 MSG). Gabriel then told him, "Because you won't believe me, you'll be unable to say a word until the day of your son's birth. Every word I've spoken to you will come true on time—*God's* time" (Luke 1:20 MSG).

And that's just what happened.

Zachariah's response to Gabriel is in direct contrast to the response of his wife's cousin Mary. Zachariah, a priest from the line of Aaron, was well-entrenched in God's scriptures and temple duties. He lived

right, followed all the laws.

Mary was only a simple peasant girl. Yet ever faithful to God, she believed every astounding thing the angel told her. She believed God would make His promise a reality. And because of her belief, she was called blessed.

Where do you fall? What do you believe when God makes you a promise—however outlandish it may seem at the time? Are you filled with doubt and uncertainty? Or do you accept God at His word?

It's good to be right with God, to know His rules, and to obey Him. But it's better to have a firm belief in God. That's what God is looking for and rewards. So when doubts creep in to your thinking process, go to God. Ask Him to continue to grow your faith. And you too will be blessed.

Lord, sometimes my thoughts are riddled with doubt.
Help me believe You'll do just as You say. In Your time. Amen.

Because I believe God will do as He says, I'm happy and blessed.

Wonderfully Gray

"I have cared for you since you were born. Yes, I carried you
before you were born. I will be your God throughout your
lifetime—until your hair is white with age. I made you, and I
will care for you. I will carry you along and save you.". . .
We are citizens of heaven. . .eagerly waiting for [Jesus Christ]
to return as our Savior. He will take our weak mortal bodies
and change them into glorious bodies like his own.
<small>ISAIAH 46:3-4; PHILIPPIANS 3:20-21 NLT</small>

There will come a time, if it hasn't already, when you catch a glimpse
of yourself in the mirror and wonder, *When did I start looking so old?*

The fact of the matter is that aging is a normal process. And although
you may not feel old on the inside, changes are definitely taking place
on the outside. What you have to be alert to are negative comments
about aging from others, for they can lead to the formation of negative
thoughts in your own mind. Thoughts such as, *I'm so old. I'm not good
for anything anymore.*

Don't believe it! You are of value to God no matter *how* old you are!
Consider Noah who became a father when he was 500 and set off in
the ark when he was 600! Abraham became a father at age 100! Moses
was 80 when he spoke to the Pharaoh.

Know that God, the "Ancient of Days" (Daniel 7:9), says the older
you get, the more wisdom and understanding you gain (Job 12:12; 32:7).

When others show honor to people with gray hair, God himself is honored (Leviticus 19:32). Although "the glory of the young is their strength; the gray hair of experience is the splendor of the old" (Proverbs 20:29 NLT).

And don't worry so much about how you look. After all, you're already a citizen of God's kingdom, awaiting Jesus. And when He comes, He'll transform your body to be just like His—glorious (Philippians 3:20-21)! So why work on what may be temporary improvements when God's got something better waiting just around the corner!

As I grow older, Lord, remind me that I am of great worth to You and others. Help me to make good use of my time so I can continue to grow in Your wisdom (Psalm 90:12). Also help me realize that although my health and spirit may weaken, You, Lord, will continue to be the strength of my heart forever (Psalm 73:26). Amen.

God values me at every age!

Promise Keepers

*Know in all your hearts and in all your souls that not one
of all the good promises the Lord your God made to you
has been broken. All have come true for you. . . .
Do not throw away your trust, for your reward will be great.
You must be willing to wait without giving up. After you
have done what God wants you to do, God will
give you what He promised you.*

JOSHUA 23:14; HEBREWS 10:35-36 NLV

It can be difficult to be patient. Especially when you live in a culture that offers instant gratification. You see something you want online, put in an order, and it's on your doorstep the next day.

Of course, not everything works like that. Especially when it comes to God's conditional promises. That's when God says that if you do this, He'll do that. Conditional promises are the opposite of *unconditional* promises of God. These promises are ones God will fulfill with no action needed on your part. One such promise would be that God will never leave you. But, here, we're mainly concerned with the conditional promises, ones that require some action—and perhaps some patience—from you.

God promises He'll never break a promise He's made to you. Jesus promises you'll receive something, if you ask; you'll find, if you seek; and the door will be opened, if you knock (Matthew 7:7-8).

So what if you've asked and have yet to receive, or sought and have

yet to find, or have knocked and the door has not yet been opened? How long can a girl wait? As long as it takes.

Remember that God is working things out, in His time. And that might take a while. Because to Him, "one day is as a thousand years. . . and a thousand years as one day" (2 Peter 3:8 ESV).

Your part is first to keep your end of the promise faithfully. The other is to be patient. Not to let a negative thought such as *God's promises will never come true for me* work its way into your mind. Instead, just keep on trusting God, knowing He has never broken a promise in His eternal life. Your Lord and Creator will come through! Promise!

Lord, I'm willing to wait. To never give up. I'm trusting You to reward me for my patience. For I know You are true to Your word! Amen!

God always keeps His promises to me!

Dreams and Desires

Cast your burden on the Lord [releasing the
weight of it] and He will sustain you. . . .
Is anyone among you afflicted (ill-treated, suffering
evil)? He should pray. Is anyone glad at heart?
He should sing praise [to God].
PSALM 55:22; JAMES 5:13 AMPC

It's one thing to be pining for a dream or desire to be fulfilled. But even worse is being taunted by someone who is *living* your dream, having already *attained* your desire. That's how it was for Hannah.

Elkanah had two wives: Hannah and Peninnah. Although he loved Hannah more, she was childless while the less-loved Peninnah had given him sons and daughters. Year after year, Peninnah would taunt, tease, and provoke Hannah because she had no children, leaving her in tears and without an appetite. Elkanah would try to console Hannah, asking if he did not mean more to her than ten sons.

Then one year during a visit to the temple, Hannah "was in distress of soul, praying to the Lord and weeping bitterly" (1 Samuel 1:10 AMPC). She vowed that if He would give her a son, she would dedicate him to God. After she poured out her soul to God, the temple priest Eli said, "Go in peace, and may the God of Israel grant your petition" (1 Samuel 1:17 AMPC). Hannah "went her way and ate, her countenance no longer sad" (1 Samuel 1:18 AMPC).

Soon afterward Hannah became pregnant with Samuel whom she dedicated to the Lord. She then praised God and went on to have five more children (1 Samuel 2:1-10, 21)!

When you feel your situation is hopeless, when your dreams seem unattainable and your desires unfulfilled, keep your cool. Patiently persevere no matter what (or who) provokes you amid the process. Then go to God. Fight your battle on your knees in prayer. Release the weight of your burden upon Him. Then rise up, leaving the situation in God's capable hands, knowing He alone will sustain you and bring you victory.

Lord, You know the desires of my heart, the dreams I am waiting to be fulfilled. Today, I am coming to You on my knees, casting my burdens upon You, and leaving them in Your hands. I rise up, determined to "trust in, lean on, and confidently rely on You" alone to bring me victory (Psalm 55:23 AMPC). Amen.

God takes my burdens and transforms them to victories!

It's All Good

"You intended to harm me, but God intended it all for good. He brought
me to this position so I could save the lives of many people." . . .
We are assured and know that [God being a partner in their labor]
all things work together and are [fitting into a plan] for
good to and for those who love God and are called
according to [His] design and purpose.
GENESIS 50:20 NLT; ROMANS 8:28 AMPC

Genesis relates the charmed life Joseph had. . .in the beginning. He was his father's favorite, wore a special coat made just for him, and dreamed that one day he'd reign over his brothers. But then, things went a little sour.

Filled with jealousy, Joseph's brothers decided to get rid of him. They ripped off his cool coat, threw him in a pit, and sold him to some traders passing by. When they went back to their father, Jacob, they showed him the tattered coat, which they'd dipped in goat's blood, and claimed Joseph had been eaten by a wild beast.

Meanwhile, Joseph was sold again in Egypt, accused of rape, and thrown into prison. Eventually, he came to the attention of Pharaoh. Pleased with Joseph's wisdom and his dream interpretations, Pharaoh made him his number two man.

Years later, Joseph met up with his brothers, telling them that although what they'd done was intended for evil, God made it work for good.

But how did Joseph keep his sanity and his faith during all those

years in servitude and prison? How did he not only hang on to his dreams but actually prosper?

Here's how: Joseph knew the Lord was with him, bringing him success in everything he did. And the people around him—his owners, prison keepers, and Pharaoh himself—knew it too (Genesis 39:2-3; 21-23). Turning things over to Joseph, they became blessed themselves!

No matter what difficulties you find yourself in, don't get behind enemy lines, believing *God is out to get me. That's why I'm going through all this trauma!* Instead, know that no matter where you are, God is with you, using you, blessing you as you stay close to and serve Him. Know that God is working *with* you, giving you the strength and energy to carry on, come what may!

Be with me, Lord, no matter what comes my way. Bless me in every situation, good and not-so-good, so that I can in turn bless those around me. Amen.

God works all things out for my good!

And Yet. . .

Is anything too hard or too wonderful for the Lord?. . .
With God nothing is ever impossible and no word from
God shall be without power or impossible of fulfillment.
GENESIS 18:14; LUKE 1:37 AMPC

When Abraham was ninety-nine, the Lord made him a promise. God told him he'd be the father of many nations—and that He'd bless his eighty-nine-year-old wife, Sarah, who would give birth to Abraham's son. Hearing this, "Abraham fell on his face and laughed and said in his heart, Shall a child be born to a man who is a hundred years old? And shall Sarah, who is ninety years old, bear a son?" (Genesis 17:17 AMPC). Can you blame him? It does sound pretty impossible. And yet. . .

Later, God came to Abraham again while Sarah was inside the tent, listening at the door. He told Abraham, "I will surely return to you when the season comes round, and behold, Sarah your wife will have a son" (Genesis 18:10 AMPC). Well past child-bearing years, "Sarah laughed to herself, saying, After I have become aged shall I have pleasure *and* delight, my lord (husband), being old also?" (Genesis 18:12 AMPC).

God couldn't believe His ears and so said, "Why did Sarah laugh. . . ? Is anything too hard or too wonderful for the Lord?" (Genesis 18:13-14 AMPC). And yet. . .

At the time God indicated, Sarah *did* give birth to a son. And as God directed, they named him Isaac, which means, "he laughs."

Have you ever read one of God's promises and laughed to yourself, thinking, *Yeah, right. Like that's ever going to happen*? If so, take note. What God promises, He will provide. There are no ifs, ands, buts, or giggles—God *will* do as He says. For there is nothing impossible for Him. Everything God says, everything He has promised His people that He will do, becomes a reality. It may take a while. After all, Abraham first heard the promise that God would make him a great nation when he was seventy-five years old (Genesis 12:1-5)! He had to wait twenty-five years for God's promise to become a reality!

Yet the fact remains, there is nothing God cannot do. And there's nothing He *will* not do to keep His promises to you. His job is to bring His words into reality. Your job is to wait in faith that He'll do it.

Mighty God, how amazing to consider that nothing—absolutely nothing—is impossible for You. I must remember that there is nothing more true and sure than a promise from You.

God's promises become my reality.

The Best-Laid Plans

Roll your works upon the Lord [commit and trust them wholly to
Him; He will cause your thoughts to become agreeable to His
will, and] so shall your plans be established and succeed. . . .
Watch your step. Use your head. Make the most of every
chance you get. . . . Don't live carelessly, unthinkingly.
Make sure you understand what the Master wants.
PROVERBS 16:3 AMPC; EPHESIANS 5:15-17 MSG

Ah, the best-laid plans. . . .

In Genesis 12, God promised Abraham that He'd make him a mighty nation. Later, God told him he'd have more descendants than he could ever count (Genesis 13). In Genesis 15, Abraham, still childless, asked God if his heir would be the son of his servant. God said no. His heir would come from his own body.

Ten years later, Sarah and Abraham were *still* waiting for a child. That's when Sarah decided to take things into her own hands.

Without running her plan by God, a barren Sarah told Abraham, "The LORD has prevented me from having children. Go and sleep with my servant. Perhaps I can have children through her" (Genesis 16:2 NLT). So Abraham did. But when Hagar became pregnant, she began lording her condition over Sarah. Sarah then blamed Abraham for the mess she created. After Abraham told her to deal with Hagar as she saw fit, Sarah began treating the girl so badly that Hagar finally ran away.

Thinking your plans never succeed? That may be true. For whenever you make plans that don't agree with God's, your plans may not only fail but cost you a huge price in the process. Only when you understand what God wants and remain patient while He's working things out will your plans flourish!

Commit and entrust all your plans to God. When you do, He'll make sure your thoughts, ideas, and strategies line up with His vision for you.

If you want to know how to figure out what God wills, dig deep into His Word. Seek out His thoughts. Then take yourself and your ideas to Him. Ask Him to help you keep on His path for you. Then, as you remain patient, checking in with Him every step of the way, you will find success—just as He planned!

Lord, I so often either lag behind or run ahead of Your plans for me. Help me to slow down, to align my plan with Yours. For then I know success will be ours!

Following God's plans, I will succeed!

God Hears

The Lord has heard and paid attention to your affliction. . . .
When the Lord saw her, He had compassion
on her and said to her, Do not weep.
GENESIS 16:11; LUKE 7:13 AMPC

Ten years had passed since God promised Sarah and Abraham they'd have a son. And still no child. Out of impatience and desperation, Sarah took things into her own hands and gave her servant Hagar to Abraham, saying, "Perhaps I can have children through her" (Genesis 16:2 NLT). Abraham slept with Hagar and she conceived. "But when Hagar knew she was pregnant, she began to treat her mistress, Sarai, with contempt" (Genesis 16:4 NLT). That's when, with Abraham's okay, Sarah began to be cruel to Hagar. So she ran away.

God found Hagar by a spring. He asked her where she came from and where she was going. Hagar, assuming a victim mentality, told Him, "I am running away from my mistress Sarai" (Genesis 16:8 AMPC).

God then told Hagar to "Go back to your mistress and [humbly] submit to her control" (Genesis 16:9 AMPC), to change her hatred of Sarah to obedience to her. But God immediately followed that with a promise: He'd give her more children than she could count. He then told Hagar she'd have a son and would call him Ishmael ("God hears") because God had listened to and answered her.

Hearing this, Hagar "called the name of the Lord Who spoke to

her, You are a God of seeing, for she said, Have I [not] even here [in the wilderness] looked upon Him Who sees me [and lived]? *Or have I here also seen [the future purposes or designs of] Him Who sees me?*" (Genesis 16:13 AMPC).

When life gets really tough, you may want to lapse into the role of playing the victim, to run away or give up. But God wants you to face your challenges and transform your attitude. To recognize He has a plan for you.

So get that *woe-is-me* thought out of your head. Turn to God. Ask what He'd have you do, where He'd have you go, even if it means staying put or taking some steps back. Allow God to transform your attitude. Recognize that He hears and sees you. He has compassion for you. And even though you might be in a hard place, He'll bless you there.

Thank You, Lord, for hearing me. Give me direction,
help me live out Your plan, then bless me wherever I land. Amen.

God hears and blesses me.

Rising Up

*"Let those who love [the Lord] be like
the sun as he rises in his power."...
You're...daughters of Day.... Act like it.
Walk out into the daylight sober, dressed up
in faith, love, and the hope of salvation.*
JUDGES 5:31 NLV; 1 THESSALONIANS 5:5, 8 MSG

If you're looking for a hero, a woman to emulate, consider Deborah. She was a homemaker, a judge, and a prophet who exuded strength, faith, and positivity.

Before the days of kings, God raised up judges to help His people. When we meet Deborah, the Israelites had been oppressed by King Jabin and his army commander Sisera's 900 chariots for twenty years.

Meanwhile, Deborah held court at home. Then one day, she sent for Barak. She told him God had commanded him to "Go to Mount Tabor and prepare for battle. Take ten companies of soldiers.... I'll take care of getting Sisera.... And I'll make sure you win the battle" (Judges 4:6-7 MSG). Barak told her he'd go but only if she, Deborah, went with him. In *All of the Women of the Bible*, Edith Deen writes, "That is one of the most unusual passages in the Bible spoken by a man to a woman. It demonstrates a general's confidence in a woman, a homebody too, who had risen to a high place in Israel largely because of her one quality, her abiding faith in God" (page 72).

Deborah told Barak she'd go with him but to "understand that with an attitude like that, there'll be no glory in it for you" (Judges 4:9-10 MSG). Then Deborah took positive action as she rose up (Judges 4:9), physically and faithfully, and went forward with Barak.

When they reached their face-off with Sisera and his chariots, Deborah encouraged Barak, saying, "Up! For this is the day when the Lord has given Sisera into your hand. Is not the Lord gone out before you?" (Judges 4:14 AMPC). In the end, God, having confused and terrified Sisera, his chariot drivers, and army, brought His people complete and ultimate victory, and under Deborah's leadership, peace for the next forty years.

Daughters of the day, don't let a negative attitude keep you down. Instead, love God. Feed your faith in His Word. And you, like Deborah, will rise up in His light and power.

Lord, as a daughter of Your great light, I rise up in Your power, knowing You will give me victory!

God gives me the power to rise up!

It Is Well

"It will be all right.... Drive on.... It is well."...
It's what we trust in but don't yet see that keeps us going.
2 KINGS 4:23-24, 26 NLV; 2 CORINTHIANS 5:7 MSG

A wealthy yet childless woman lived in Shunem. Every once in a while, when the prophet Elisha passed by, she'd insist he come into her home for a meal. Then she suggested to her husband that they make a room in their home, just for Elisha.

Sometime later, during one of Elisha's visits, he decided to do something to repay the Shunammite's kindness. So he told her next year, she'd have a son. And she did.

The boy grew over the next ten or twelve years, becoming the apple of her eye. But then one day he fainted while in the fields. His father had a servant carry the child to his mother. She held him on her lap until noon, and then he died. She laid him on Elisha's bed, then went out, and told her husband to get her a servant and a donkey so she could ride out to find Elisha. The husband asked, "Why will you go to him today?" (2 Kings 4:23 NLV). Her only response was, "It will be all right." Then she said to her servant, "Drive on. Do not slow down for me unless I tell you" (2 Kings 4:24 NLV).

When Elisha saw the Shunammite woman coming, he sent his servant to run to her and find out if anything was wrong. She responded, "It is well." Eventually, Elisha went into her home, ministered to the boy, and

brought him back to life.

In what must have been the worst day of this woman's life, her faith never faltered. Unwilling to give in to fear, she allowed her faith to drive her on. She never once voiced the words, "My son is dead." Instead, she kept calmly moving forward, seeking out the man of God. She firmly believed that God in His goodness would work a miracle. And He did.

Allow your trust in God to keep you calm no matter what crises you may face. Walk by faith, convinced He will make things right. As you do, God will work miracles.

I trust in You, Lord, not in what I see.
Because of You, all is well with my soul. Amen.

Because I walk by faith, all is well.

No Looking Back

One of the angels ordered, "Run for your lives!
And don't look back or stop."... But Lot's wife looked
back...and she turned into a pillar of salt....
Remember what happened to Lot's wife! If you grasp
and cling to life on your terms, you'll lose it, but if you
let that life go, you'll get life on God's terms.
GENESIS 19:17, 26 NLT; LUKE 17:32-33 MSG

The older people get, the more they hearken back to the good old days, seeing their past only through rose-colored glasses. Others become so enamored of where they are in the present that they cannot see moving out into the future. Yet all this attachment to the recollections of the past or the comfort of the present can keep a woman from moving forward, even when God is urging her on. She tries to deter His plan, thinking to herself, *I'm just not ready.* Or, *Why leave now? I have everything I'd want in the world, right here.* Yet it's just this kind of thinking that can lead to peril. Remember Lot's wife.

Mr. and Mrs. Lot lived in Sodom when two angels stopped by for a visit. They came with a warning: This city, as well as that of Gomorrah, was so evil that God intended to destroy it. Completely. They needed to get out—quickly!

Unable to convince anyone to come with them, Lot and his family were hurried out by the angels. When Lot continued to hesitate, not

wanting to leave his home and possessions, the angels grabbed the hands of all family members and hurried them away, literally telling them to "Run for your lives!"

They finally reached safety when the sun started to rise. That's when God rained down fire and sulfur onto the cities, annihilating them. But Lot's wife couldn't resist. She looked back at what she'd once had and became a pillar of salt. Immovable. Because she could not let go of her life, unable to live it on God's terms, she became forever rooted to that spot.

Jesus makes it clear that you need to let go of what you have or have had in this world. Only then can you find the true life. The one you live for the God who loves and wants you—all of you.

I know my true life is living in You, Lord. Help me to detach from all that would hinder my moving forward. For You are my true treasure, my forever home. In Jesus' name, amen.

Living in and for God alone, I find my true life.

An Adventure in Success

"You shall go. . . . He will send His Angel before you.". . .
God's Spirit beckons. There are things to do and places to go!
GENESIS 24:4, 7 AMPC; ROMANS 8:14 MSG

What's your self-talk like when you're stepping out of your comfort zone? What thoughts run through your head when you're beginning a new journey? What prayers do you say before, during, and after you follow God's promptings?

When Abraham was old, he gave his servant a commission: Go back to my country and find a wife for my son Isaac. The servant raised some doubts, a few what-ifs: "What if the woman won't come back with me? Maybe I should take your son with me?"

But Abraham told him Isaac was to stay home. Then he reassured his servant, saying, God "will send His Angel before you, and you will take a wife there for my son" (Genesis 24:7 AMPC).

So the servant went off. When he got to Abraham's former homeland, he did something very important. He prayed, "O Lord, God of my master Abraham, I pray You, cause me to meet with good success today" (Genesis 24:12 AMPC). Then he told God exactly where he was and asked God to point out the bride-to-be.

When Rebekah appeared, she was literally an answer to the servant's prayer, prompting him to bow down and praise God. He blessed God for dealing so kindly with Abraham, then said, "As for me, going on the

way [of obedience and faith] the Lord led me to the house of my master's kinsmen" (Genesis 24:27 AMPC).

Abraham's servant had taken his master's words to heart—"The Lord, in Whose presence I walk [habitually], will send His Angel with you and prosper your way" (Genesis 24:40 AMPC) and so you will find what you seek. He so believed these words that before he'd even finished praying in his heart, his answer arrived.

God's angel goes before you when you walk His way, aligned with His plan. So any thoughts of failure, creeping doubts, or agonizing what-ifs have no place in your journey. As you *live by His words and pray in His presence*, God will lead you just where you need to be and answer your prayer for success. So go, do, be, live, pray, walk, praise. God's spirit beckons!

Thank You, Lord, for sending Your angel before me whenever and wherever I go. Walking in Your presence, I know You will prosper my way! Amen.

I walk with confidence because God goes before me!

Getting Under Instead of Around God

Whoever walks in integrity walks securely, but he who
makes his ways crooked will be found out. . . .
God is not mocked, for whatever one sows,
that will he also reap.

PROVERBS 10:9; GALATIANS 6:7 ESV

Rebekah's story begins well. She was kind to Abraham's servant and his camels. She didn't hesitate when asked to travel to an unfamiliar land and marry the forty-year-old Isaac. The only thing lacking in their life was children. So "Isaac prayed to the LORD. . . . The LORD granted his prayer, and Rebekah his wife conceived" (Genesis 25:21 ESV).

When the children within Rebekah started struggling with each other, she was the first woman to "inquire of the LORD" (Genesis 25:22 ESV). God said, "Two nations are in your womb, two peoples butting heads while still in your body. One people will overpower the other, and the older will serve the younger" (Genesis 25:23 MSG). And God was right!

When Rebekah gave birth, Esau appeared first, Jacob second. And favorites were chosen. Isaac, who loved game, favored the hunter Esau. And Rebekah favored the quiet homebody Jacob.

After Jacob bribed Esau into giving up his birthright as the firstborn son, Rebekah overheard Isaac telling Esau to hunt some game, prepare it for him, then bring it to him so he could eat it before blessing Esau. Rebekah, wanting to make sure *Jacob* got Isaac's blessing, began to plot,

determined to work her will and disregard God's.

Jacob wasn't sure his mother's plan would fool his father. He feared Isaac would end up cursing instead of blessing him. Undeterred, Rebekah said, "Let your curse be on me, my son; only obey" (Genesis 27:13 ESV). So Jacob fooled his father and gained his brother's blessing as well as his birthright but had to leave before Esau killed him. Rebekah never saw Jacob again. She spent her last years with a husband and son who no longer trusted her.

Rebekah put her love for Jacob above her love of God, her fear before her faith, her will and plan before God's will and plan.

When thoughts of getting around God enter into your mind or fears prompt you to consider plans of deception, stop. Then pray for God to increase your faith and trust in Him.

Lord, help me run all my thoughts and plans by You when fears arise or impatience peaks. In You alone, I trust my and my loved one's futures. In Jesus' name, amen.

I find my blessings in trusting God's plan.

For Such a Time

If you keep silent at this time, relief and deliverance shall arise for the Jews from elsewhere, but you and your father's house will perish. And who knows but that you have come to the kingdom for such a time as this and for this very occasion? . . . "If anyone wants to be My follower, he must forget about himself. He must take up his cross and follow Me."

ESTHER 4:14 AMPC; MATTHEW 16:24, NLV

During times of crises, the mind and emotions start to reel. Thoughts like, *What if the worst happens?* begin coursing through the brain. Imaginary scenarios, which seem so real but may never come to life, begin to play out in the head.

Esther was an orphan, a Jewish exile, who became the queen of Persia. During her reign, the king's administrator, Haman, launched a campaign to annihilate the Jews. This was his payback to Mordecai, Esther's cousin, who would not bow to Haman but only to God.

When Mordecai sent word to Esther that evil was afoot, encouraging her to plead with the king on her people's behalf, she hesitated. She told Mordecai that anyone who went to the king without first being called could be put to death (her worst-case scenario).

In response, Mordecai told Esther that if she kept quiet, "God will call someone else to rise up while you and your family will be destroyed anyway. Who knows? Maybe God has put you in your current position

so you could do this very thing."

Esther sent a message back to Mordecai, telling him to have all Jews within the kingdom hold a fast for her for three days. Then she'd go to the king, even though it was against the law, saying, "If I die, I die" (Esther 4:16 NLV).

Three days later, Esther set self aside, plucked up her courage, put on her robes, and went to see the king. Instead of her being killed, he was putty in her hands. "What's your desire, Queen Esther? . . . Ask and it's yours. . . !" (Esther 5:3 MSG). In the end, the Jews were saved.

When crises come into your life, don't let fears and imaginary worst-case scenarios keep you from answering God's call. Instead, forget about yourself. Look to God. And consider: perhaps you are here for such a time as this.

Give me the strength and courage, Lord, to forget
about myself and answer Your call. Amen.

I will not fear, for God has put me here for such a time as this.

Finding Refuge

*"Wherever you go, I will go; wherever you live, I will live.
Your people will be my people, and your God will be my God."...
We are the house of the living God. God has said, "I will live
in them and will walk among them. I will be their
God and they will be My people."*

RUTH 1:16 NLT; 2 CORINTHIANS 6:16 NLV

When life doesn't go the way you think it should, when you feel as if you've been left with nothing, it's only natural to seek some sort of refuge.

Ruth 1 presents Naomi, a woman who'd left drought-stricken Judah and moved to fertile Moab with her husband and two boys. There her sons married Moabites Ruth and Orpah. And there Naomi's husband and sons died, leaving behind three childless widows.

When Naomi heard Judah's drought was over, she began the long trek home with her daughters-in-law following. But seeing no good future for them with her, Naomi entreated them to go back to their fathers. Naomi then revealed her mistaken mind-set. Interpreting her circumstances as a result of God's unhappiness with her, Naomi said, "Things are far more bitter for me than for you, because the LORD himself has raised his fist against me" (Ruth 1:13 NLT).

Hearing those words, Orpah tearfully turned back. But Ruth revealed *her* refuge was God, pledging she would go wherever Naomi went, Naomi's God would be her God, and nothing would ever separate them.

After a long journey, Ruth and Naomi arrived in Bethlehem. There Naomi took her resentment against God even further, announcing to her neighbors, "The Almighty has made life very bitter for me. I went away full, but the LORD has brought me home empty. Why call me Naomi when the LORD has caused me to suffer and sent such tragedy upon me?" (Ruth 1:20-21 NLT).

Meanwhile Ruth, in her efforts to support herself and Naomi, gleaned in Boaz's fields. He'd heard how much she'd done for Naomi, leaving her own home and family to live among strangers. So he blessed Ruth: "May the LORD. . .under whose wings you have come to take refuge, reward you" (Ruth 2:12 NLT).

Naomi, Orpah, and Ruth all suffered great losses, but their thoughts led them to seek different refuges. Naomi's led to bitterness. Orpah's to her family and their gods. Ruth's to her loving God. Where might your thoughts lead you?

Help me, Lord, to pay attention to my self-talk,
to ensure I seek my refuge in You alone.

My refuge and hope are in God alone.

Strength of Mind

"If we are thrown into the blazing furnace, the God whom we
serve is able to save us. He will rescue us from your power. . . .
But even if he doesn't. . .we will never serve your gods
or worship the gold statue you have set up.". . .
They. . .warned them that they were on no account ever again
to speak or teach in the name of Jesus. But Peter and John spoke
right back, "Whether it's right in God's eyes to listen to you
rather than to God, you decide. As for us, there's no
question—we can't keep quiet."
DANIEL 3:17-18 NLT; ACTS 4:18-20 MSG

Daniel and his three friends—Shadrach, Meshach, and Abednego—were taken from Jerusalem to serve in Nebuchadnezzar's palace in Babylon. From the beginning, they refused to be assimilated into their enemy's culture. Because they stayed true to God, He blessed them with education and wisdom, far more than that of their pagan counterparts.

But Daniel's friends' commitment to God was truly tested when Nebuchadnezzar had a golden statue made in his image and commanded all people to bow down and worship it. Those refusing would be cast into a blazing furnace.

When Shadrach, Meshach, and Abednego would not worship Nebuchadnezzar's image, he became enraged. He asked them who, if anyone, would be able to save them from the fire? They answered, "Our

God. But if He doesn't, He doesn't. Either way, we won't serve you."

Furious, Nebuchadnezzar had the furnace turned up higher than usual and the three men bound up and thrown in. Yet when he looked into the flames, he didn't see three men walking around in the fire but four! And the fourth one looked like the son of God! The king ordered the three men to come out of the furnace. When they did, he noticed the fire hadn't touched them or their clothes. They didn't even smell like smoke! Nebuchadnezzar then praised their rescuing God—and promoted them to even higher positions!

When you refuse to be conformed to this world and allow God to transform your mind, you will develop a rock-solid, fireproof faith. One that will enable you to stay true to God, no matter what. Regardless of how things work out, whether you're burned or not, you can be sure God is with you—in the fire and out.

---

*Lord, I want a fireproof faith! Transform my mind as
I stick close to You today and every day. Amen.*

God sticks with me when I stick with Him.

Vision Check

If the Lord delights in us, then He will bring us into this land and give it to us. . . . Only do not rebel against the Lord, neither fear the people of the land, for they are bread for us. Their defense and the shadow [of protection] is removed from over them, but the Lord is with us. Fear them not. . . .
Let us run with patient endurance. . .the appointed course. . .set before us, looking away [from all that will distract] to Jesus.
NUMBERS 14:8-9; HEBREWS 12:1-2 AMPC

Sometimes the mind may play tricks on you, skewing your vision. Add some fear to the mix, and the imagination goes wild. Here's a case in point:

The Israelites had recently escaped from Egypt. After several days in the wilderness, Moses sent twelve spies to check out the land God had promised His people, a land flowing with milk and honey. When they came back, Moses and the people received conflicting reports.

The spies had gone into the land. It did flow with milk and honey. BUT the people who lived there were HUGE and STRONG. GIANTS. And their cities IMPREGNABLE.

But then Caleb spoke up: "Let's go up and take the land—now. We can do it" (Numbers 13:30 MSG). Joshua agreed.

But the other ten spies said, "We can't attack those people; they're way stronger than we are. . . . Everybody we saw was huge. . . . We felt like

grasshoppers. And they looked down on us as if we were grasshoppers" (Numbers 13:31-33 MSG).

Next thing you know, the people were crying and grumbling. They wanted to head back to slavery in Egypt, wishing they'd died there rather than wandering freely in this wilderness. Such talk so angered God that He said none of the grumblers would ever see the Promised Land. But Joshua and Caleb would.

When you come up against obstacles, check your vision. Do you see your difficulties as something bigger than God? Do you feel or see yourself as small and weak as a grasshopper when you stand before them? If so, go to God and ask for a different spirit and a new line of thought. No obstacle is bigger or mightier than God. With Him, you can do anything!

Sometimes, Lord, when I come up against a challenge,
I see myself as inadequate and small. Help me to get a new
perspective. To remember I can do anything with You! Amen.

God is bigger and mightier than any obstacle.

The Formula for Success

"In the same way I was with Moses, I'll be with you.
I won't give up on you; I won't leave you. Strength! Courage!"...
God assured us, "I'll never let you down, never walk off and leave you."
JOSHUA 1:5-6; HEBREWS 13:5 MSG

Moses had died, never having made it into the Promised Land. Now his longtime assistant, Joshua, was to lead God's people on to the land of milk and honey. So the first thing God did was give Joshua not just a pep talk but a formula for success.

First, God wanted Joshua to get it through his head that He was with Him. There was no way He'd ever leave him or abandoned him.

Second, God told Joshua to "be strong and courageous" (Joshua 1:6 NLT), because he was the one who'd lead God's people in conquering the Promised Land.

Third, God repeated that Joshua should be "strong and very courageous," to obey God's instructions, and "not deviate from them.... Then you will be successful in everything you do" (Joshua 1:7 NLT).

Fourth, Joshua was to study God's book of Law. Not just once in a while but continually. He was to "meditate on it day and night...to obey everything written in it. Only then will you prosper and succeed in all you do" (Joshua 1:8 NLT).

Finally, God commanded Joshua to "be strong and courageous! Do not be afraid or discouraged. For the LORD your God is with you

wherever you go" (Joshua 1:9 NLT).

Joshua followed these guidelines and, in the end, was successful.

What God willed Joshua to do is what He wills you to do. God wants all thoughts of abandonment, weakness, fear, and discouragement out of your mind. He wants them replaced with the knowledge that He is with you and will never leave you. He tells you over and over again to be brave, be strong. God wants you to read His Word. To meditate on it day and night. To allow His words to be the dialogue running in your head. God wants you to obey His instructions. When you do this, you too will have success. To your pleasure and God's glory!

Thank You, God, for never giving up on me. For always walking with me. Help me to be brave and strong. Give me the willingness to obey You in every way, beginning with reading and meditating on Your Word, replacing my thoughts with Yours. In Jesus' name, I pray.

God alone gives me success!

Ignoring Can Be Bliss

The man who is right and good...will not be afraid of bad
news. His heart is strong because he trusts in the Lord....
Overhearing but ignoring what they said, Jesus said to the ruler
of the synagogue, Do not be seized with alarm and
struck with fear; only keep on believing.
PSALM 112:6-7 NLV; MARK 5:36 AMPC

Jairus, a leader of a synagogue, fell down at the feet of Jesus. He told Him his twelve-year-old daughter was dying. "Come and lay your hands on her, so that she may be made well and live" (Mark 5:23 ESV). So Jesus went with him, a crowd following them from behind.

Along the way, Jesus got sidetracked into healing a woman with an issue of blood. While Jesus had a conversation with the now-healed woman, men from Jairus's house told him, "Your daughter is dead. There's no use troubling the Teacher now" (Mark 5:35 NLT). Overhearing their remarks, Jesus told Jairus, "Don't listen to them; just trust me" (Mark 5:36 MSG).

Jesus then left the crowd behind, taking only three of His disciples with Him to Jairus's house. There He encountered many people weeping and wailing. Jesus asked why there was all this hubbub. The child wasn't dead, just sleeping. The crowd only laughed at Him.

Leaving the snickers of the mourners behind, Jesus, the child's parents, and the three disciples went into the girl's room. Taking her

by the hand, Jesus said, " 'Little girl, get up!' And the girl, who was twelve years old, immediately stood up and walked around! They were overwhelmed" (Mark 5:42 NLT).

Who knows what would've happened if Jairus had listened to those telling him his child was dead or if he'd lost his trust in Jesus.

Sometimes ignoring the faithless, mocking, and disparaging words of others, as well as some of the fear-filled voices in your own head, can lead to bliss. Such comments and thoughts can be as unpredictable as shifting sands. Instead of heeding those voices, replace them with the rock-solid words of Jesus: "Keep on believing" (Mark 5:36 AMPC).

Thank You, Lord, for this reminder. That no matter what others say,
You want me to keep on believing in You, trusting in You. Thus,
I will not fear bad news, wrong words, within or without.
I know my heart is strong because I trust in You. Amen.

I will not fear but keep on believing.

About Issues

I will cure them and will reveal to them the abundance
of peace (prosperity, security, stability) and truth. . . .
She came up behind Him in the throng and touched His garment,
for she kept saying, If I only touch His garments, I shall be
restored to health. And immediately her flow of
blood was dried up at the source.
JEREMIAH 33:6; MARK 5:27-29 AMPC

For twelve years, a woman had been hemorrhaging blood. She'd gone to numerous doctors. They'd taken her money but couldn't heal her. Instead of getting better, she was getting worse.

Yet she'd heard about Jesus. So she determined to approach Him under the cover of a crowd. "She came up behind Him in the throng and touched His garment, for she kept saying, If I only touch His garments, I shall be restored to health" (Mark 5:27-28 AMPC). As soon as she touched the hem of his coat, her flow of blood stopped. But she wasn't home free yet!

Realizing healing power had flowed out of Him, Jesus asked who'd touched Him. Frightened, the woman fell down before Jesus and explained what she'd done. But instead of chastising her, Jesus said, "Daughter, your faith (your trust and confidence in Me, springing from faith in God) has restored you to health. Go in (into) peace and be continually healed *and* freed" (Mark 5:34 AMPC).

This woman had tried remedy after remedy. She was sore of body, lacking energy, spent of money, looking for relief, and feeling lost in the crowd. But she knew Jesus was the answer. She kept thinking, telling herself, *If only I reach out to Him, I'll be restored.* And it was these faith-filled thoughts, her confidence in Christ, that brought her healing!

When you've got an issue, when you need restoration, consider your self-talk, what you've been saying to yourself. Revise your inner dialogue where needed. Then gather up your now faith-filled and empowered thoughts and reach out to Jesus. Believe He has the remedy, the healing, the peace, the answer, the truth you've been looking for. And you'll get it!

Lord, I have issues. I realize I've been looking for a remedy in all the wrong places. Guide me on this journey to restoration in You. Change up my inner dialogue, aligning it to what You would have me hope, expect, and believe, knowing as I trust in You, I will receive the healing I need. Amen.

My faith in God restores me.

Be Ye Transformed

Those who return evil for good will meet their own evil returning. . . .
Repay no one evil for evil, but take thought for what is honest and
proper and noble [aiming to be above reproach]
in the sight of everyone. . . . Do not let yourself be overcome
by evil, but overcome (master) evil with good.
PROVERBS 17:13 MSG; ROMANS 12:17, 21 AMPC

Abigail and her wealthy husband Nabal were an odd couple. While she's described as "a woman of good understanding, and beautiful. . .the man was rough and evil" (1 Samuel 25:3 AMPC).

Their differences were amplified when David came onto the scene. While in the wilderness, he and his men had been like a wall of protection around Nabal's shepherds. In return for this kindness, David asked Nabal for some provisions. But that brute refused. In response, David decided to attack Nabal's household.

When Abigail's servant divulged the situation, she immediately gathered provisions and sent them ahead with her servants. She then followed on her own donkey. When Abigail finally reached David and his men, she admitted her husband was wicked and foolish, for that's what his name means. But, she said, she had no idea what had been going on and was hoping these supplies would appease David, whom she described as one whose life was "safe in the care of the LORD your God, secure in his treasure pouch" (1 Samuel 25:29 NLT). David *was* appeased and sent

her back home in peace.

That night, Nabal had a feast and got drunk. So Abigail waited until the next morning to tell him what'd happened. Hearing her news, Nabal suffered a stroke. Ten days later he died. Before long, David sent for and married Abigail.

In *Through the Bible Day by Day*, F. B. Meyer writes, "Never let the evil disposition of one mate hinder the devotion and grace of the other. Never let the difficulties of your home lead you to abdicate your throne. Do not step down to the level of your circumstances, but lift them to your own high calling in Christ. 'Be not conformed. . .but be ye transformed' (Romans 12:2 KJV)."

When someone close to you has or acquires a bad disposition, don't allow it to change you. Don't let their ways become your ways. Instead, stay close to God, allowing Him to help you not conform but be transformed.

---

*Lord, no matter who I'm with, help me to become
more like You and less like them. Amen.*

I rise with Christ above my difficulties.

One Thing

I'm asking GOD for one thing, only one thing:
To live with him in his house my whole life long.
I'll contemplate his beauty; I'll study at his feet. . . .
Mary, sat at the Lord's feet, listening to what he taught. . . .
"My dear Martha, you are worried and upset over all these details!
There is only one thing worth being concerned about. Mary has
discovered it, and it will not be taken away from her."

PSALM 27:4 MSG; LUKE 10:39, 41-42 NLT

One day, Martha invited Jesus to dinner in the home she shared with her sister Mary. While Martha was "overly occupied and too busy" (Luke 10:40 AMPC), running around, preparing dinner, setting the table, serving the food, etc., Mary sat at Jesus' feet and listened to what He was teaching His followers.

All these distractions kept Martha away from hearing Jesus' message. So far away that finally she "stepped in, interrupting them" (Luke 10:40 MSG). She then started whining to Jesus, saying, "Master, don't you care that my sister has abandoned the kitchen to me? Tell her to lend me a hand" (Luke 10:40 MSG).

That's when Jesus set Martha straight. He told her, "You're fussing far too much and getting yourself worked up over nothing" (Luke 10:41 MSG). Jesus made it clear her sister Mary had made the better choice. Only "one thing" here is important, and that's to listen to and learn from Him.

Women had and continue to have a special place in Jesus' ministry and heart. He wants them to study His words, sit at His feet, and listen to Him. He wants them to have an intimate relationship with Him, not be so distracted by other things—even if those "other things" are serving Him!

Jesus wants you to not just *seek* "one thing" but to "inquire for, *and* [insistently] require" it. And that one thing is dwelling " [in His presence] all the days" of your life. There you will "gaze upon the beauty. . .of the Lord and. . .meditate. . .in His temple" (Psalm 27:4 AMPC). For such willing and dedicated seekers can and will be transformed by Jesus.

Today, Lord, I welcome You into my home. Here I sit at Your beautiful feet, listening to Your words, Your teachings. As You fill my heart with Your presence and Your love, all distractions fade away. This is the one thing I long to do. Amen.

I choose to do one thing: sit at Jesus' feet.

Casting Off

*The Lord has anointed and qualified me. . .to proclaim liberty
to the [physical and spiritual] captives and the opening of
the prison and of the eyes to those who are bound. . . .
Let us strip off and throw aside every encumbrance (unnecessary
weight) and that sin which so readily (deftly and cleverly) clings to and
entangles us, and let us run with patient endurance and steady and
active persistence the appointed course of the race that
is set before us, looking away [from all that will distract] to Jesus.*
ISAIAH 61:1; HEBREWS 12:1-2 AMPC

Jesus and His disciples were walking out of Jericho, followed by a huge crowd. When Bartimaeus, a blind beggar, sitting on the side of the road, heard Jesus was heading his way, he yelled out, asking Jesus to have mercy on him.

Hearing his cries, Jesus stopped. He told the others, "Tell him to come here."

So they yelled to Bartimaeus, telling him to gather his courage and come over because Jesus was calling him. That's when Bartimaeus, "threw off his coat" (Mark 10:50 NLV), jumped up, and ran to Jesus.

Jesus asked, "What do you want me to do for you?" Bartimaeus said, "I want to see!"

Jesus, touching the man only with His voice, said, "Go your way; your faith has healed you" (Mark 10:52 AMPC). And "in that very instant he

recovered his sight and followed Jesus" (Mark 10:52 MSG).

Knowing He would soon be facing crucifixion, Jesus was still attuned to the sick, blind, helpless, and hopeless living on the edge of society. Hearing a sightless man's call, Jesus stopped. In His tracks. To ask a trusting blind man what he wanted Him to do for him.

The blind Bartimaeus knew what he wanted. And to get it, he threw off his coat, so it wouldn't trip him up or make him stumble on his way to Jesus.

In the days ahead, consider what might be standing in your way to transformation. What might you need to "throw off" so you can run to Jesus un-entangled? What would you like Him to do for you?

Show me, Jesus, what might be keeping me from being totally transformed by You. Help me remove any obstacles standing in my way of reaching You, to rid myself of any distractions that might veer me off course. Then, Lord, when I reach You, help me make clear my desires. In Your sweet and precious name I pray, amen.

I'm casting aside all else to reach Jesus.

Pride and Preconceptions

LORD, my heart is not proud; my eyes are not haughty. I don't concern
myself with matters too great or too awesome for me to grasp.
Instead, I have calmed and quieted myself, like a weaned
child who no longer cries for its mother's milk. . . .
Unless you repent (change, turn about) and become like
little children [trusting, lowly, loving, forgiving],
you can never enter the kingdom of heaven.
PSALM 131:1-2 NLT; MATTHEW 18:3 AMPC

Naaman, a mighty man and commander of the Syrian army, was a leper. On the advice of his wife's servant—a girl who'd been captured from Israel—he sought out the prophet Elisha for a cure.

Naaman stood outside Elisha's door in Israel, awaiting an audience with the man of God. But instead of seeing the commander, Elisha sent out a messenger who said, "Go and wash yourself seven times in the Jordan River. Then your skin will be restored, and you will be healed" (2 Kings 5:10 NLT).

The outraged Naaman stalked away. Muttering under his breath, he ticked off the list of what his now-shattered expectations had been: he'd thought that Elisha would meet him, an important man, face-to-face and that Elisha would wave his hand, call on God, and the leprosy would vanish. But none of those things happened!

Fortunately, Naaman's officers were around to give him some good

advice, including the idea that he should *just humbly trust and obey* the man of God. So Naaman followed his men's counsel as well as Elisha's prescription—and "his skin became as healthy as the skin of a young child" (2 Kings 5:14 NLT).

God wants His followers to be like little children—humble, trusting, obedient, and convinced He knows best—even if His directions sound a little strange, or not strange enough! But adults are often prideful and rebellious, swamped with preconceived notions of how God will answer their prayers, all of which may preclude them from receiving their desires.

Today, consider what preconceived notions or pride may be keeping you from receiving and following God's instructions. Then ask Him to transform you into the little girl He'd always dreamed you'd be.

Cradle me in Your arms, Lord. Bring to my mind anything that may be keeping me from humbly obeying You and trusting You. Show me where I may be blocking out Your solutions because they don't match with the ones I have in mind. Amen.

I trust God's remedies for life.

All Goes Well

You shall love the Lord your God with all your [mind and] heart
and with your entire being and with all your might. And these
words which I am commanding you this day shall
be [first] in your [own] minds and hearts. . . .
This is the great (most important, principal) and first
commandment. And a second is like it: You shall
love your neighbor as [you do] yourself.
DEUTERONOMY 6:5-6; MATTHEW 22:38-39 AMPC

Worry. It can sap the life out of you.

Perhaps you're suffering from anxiety or stress around your finances, job, health, or relationships. And you just can't figure out how to get off the fear train as constant what-ifs seem to have laid a permanent track down in your mind. You start thinking that if you could just come up with a solution, *you* can fix things. *Then* you'll have the time and energy to live a godly life.

Yet in God's eyes, that kind of thinking is *all* wrong. For He *commands* you, first and foremost, to love Him—with all your mind and heart, with your entire being, and with all your might! Why? So that all "may go well with you" (Deuteronomy 6:18 AMPC). For when you love God with *all* your mind, heart, soul, and strength, you'll find yourself automatically obeying Him and all the other commandments. All that will then lead to doing the right thing and all going well! For God knows that when you

let worry consume your mind, heart, and soul while He remains on your back burner, you'll be prone to making bad choices, wrong decisions. And that's the exact opposite of what God wants for you.

To God's greatest commandment, Jesus adds a second: love your neighbor as yourself (an echo of words God first proclaimed in Leviticus 19:18). Following this command will put you on the track of responding with compassion to others and yourself, potentially solving a myriad of problems before they even start!

As you give God's greatest commandments first place in your mind and full coverage in your heart, you'll discover there's no need or room for worry. Your thoughts will be so transformed in, by, and with love, that all will go well and all what-ifs will take flight.

Lord, transform me into a woman who wants nothing more than to love You, myself, and others—with all I am! Amen!

Loving God, myself, and others, all goes well!

Taking a Leap

"I am the LORD your God, who brought you up out of the
land of Egypt. Open your mouth wide, and I will fill it." . . .
Without faith it is impossible to please him, for whoever
would draw near to God must believe that he exists
and that he rewards those who seek him.
PSALM 81:10; HEBREWS 11:6 ESV

Author Margaret Shepard wrote, "Sometimes your only available transportation is a leap of faith." That's what the prophet Elijah learned.

After Elijah told King Ahab there'd be no more rain for a while, God told the prophet to hide in the wilderness. Then He said, "You shall drink from the brook, and"—now here comes the big leap of faith—"I have commanded the ravens to feed you there" (1 Kings 17:4 ESV). Ravens? Really, God? Yet the next verse reads, "So [Elijah] went and did according to the word of the LORD" (1 King 17:5 ESV). And there ravens brought him bread and meat in the morning and again at night! Elijah never doubted—and so received the miracle!

Elijah's amazing leap of faith not only continued but gave a widow the opportunity to join the jump! When Elijah's brook dried up, God told him to go to Zarephath. "Behold, I have commanded a widow there to feed you" (1 Kings 17:9 ESV). So Elijah once more "arose and went" (1 Kings 17:10 ESV). When he got to the village gates, he saw a widow collecting sticks. He asked her to bring him some water. On her way to get it, Elijah

asked her to bring him bread as well. That's when she revealed that all she had was a handful of flour and a bit of oil. Her plan was to make, then share this last bit of bread before she and her son died.

Elijah responded, "No worries. Just go and make the bread for me. Then for yourself. Because God says that during this drought, you'll never run out of flour and oil." So the widow took her leap of faith. She went and did as Elijah said. And God remained true to His word!

When God asks you to take a leap of faith, don't allow any thoughts of disbelief to creep into your mind. Keep seeking, believing you'll be rewarded with a miracle, and you *will* be!

Lord, I believe in You! Show me where
You would have me leap! Amen.

Because I believe, God will reward me!

Motive, Alignment, and Timing

Every man's way is right in his own eyes,
but the Lord knows the hearts. . . .
You don't have what you want because you
don't ask God for it. And even when you ask,
you don't get it because your motives are all wrong.

PROVERBS 21:2 NLV; JAMES 4:2-3 NLT

You've been praying for the same thing over and over again. And still your prayers go unanswered. So you stop asking. Or if you *do* ask, your heart isn't in it. Perhaps you're thinking God doesn't want you to be happy or He's too busy, so you stop praying altogether, except for short SOS prayers. Perhaps it's time to reconsider your thoughts around prayer. To examine your personal motive, the alignment of your desires with God's, and His timing.

Let's begin with some basic mind-blowing facts: God *does* want to give you your heart's desires (Psalm 37:4). He *is* listening (1 Peter 3:12; 1 John 5:15). He *does* want you to ask for what you want and need. When God appeared to the young King Solomon, the first thing He said was, "What do you want? Ask, and I will give it to you!" (1 Kings 3:5 NLT).

Now go deeper. Realize that when you ask God for something, He wants your motives to be pure. In 1 Kings 3:5-15, Solomon asked God for wisdom, so he could rule his people well. Because Solomon's motives were pure—no requests for long life or wealth—God gave him not only what

he asked for but what he *hadn't* asked for: riches, honor, and a long life!

Realize that if you ask God for something that's not in line with what He wants for you or is outside His plan for you, you're not going to see that prayer answered. In Genesis 17:18, Abraham asked for Ishmael to be his heir. But since that prayer wasn't part of God's plan or promise, it remained unanswered.

The timing also must be right. You may be asking for things you're not ready for. Perhaps you have a bit of growing to do. Or things are still being prepared.

So change up those wrong ideas about prayer. Examine your motive. Make sure your will is aligned with God's. And consider God's timing. Then pray away!

Lord, show me what You desire for me. Align my will and plans
with Yours, knowing You will answer in Your time. Amen.

God hears and answers prayers asked with pure motives,
aligned with His will, and in His timing.

Not a Scratch

*Daniel. . .prayed three times a day, just as he
had always done, giving thanks to his God. . . .
In the morning before the sun was up, Jesus went to
a placewhere He could be alone. He prayed there.*
DANIEL 6:10 NLT; MARK 1:35 NLV

Daniel, a Jew, had been captured and exiled to Babylon. There, against all odds, he clung to his faith. He also continued praying morning, noon, and night. As the years passed, kings continually promoted him because his God-given wisdom and intelligence was obvious. This made other leaders extremely jealous. So one day, wanting to take him down, they began looking for some evidence of corruption in him. But it seemed his only weakness was being extremely faithful to God.

So to trip up Daniel, the clever officials asked the king to issue an edict saying that "for the next thirty days any person who prays to anyone, divine or human—except to you, Your Majesty—will be thrown into the den of lions" (Daniel 6:7 NLT). King Darius agreed.

Yet even after he'd learned the edict had been signed into law, Daniel *still* went home and prayed, "just as he had always done" (Daniel 6:10 NLT). He did not allow a human's will to override God's.

Spying Daniel praying, the jealous officials ran to tell the king. And Daniel was thrown into the lions' den. But he survived, much to the joy of the king, because, "God sent his angel to shut the lions' mouths so

that they would not hurt me, for I have been found innocent in his sight" (Daniel 6:22 NLT). To top it off, "not a scratch was found on him, for he had trusted in his God" (Daniel 6:23 NLT).

Even though Daniel was living in a pagan country, he never conformed to its ways. He always stayed faithful to his God and his routine of prayer—even when doing so might mean losing his life.

Author Janette Oke said, "A quiet morning with a loving God puts the events of the upcoming day into proper perspective." That is very true. Jesus knew that. So did Daniel. Yet it's also true that *any*time you pray—morning, noon, and night (Psalm 55:16-17)—not only transforms your thoughts and outlook but boosts your faith and trust in God! That, in turn, ensures God will deliver you—without a scratch!

Help me grow in my commitment to spending time with You, Lord. For this I pray! Amen.

Prayer gives me my mighty God's perspective.

Straightened Out

Every valley shall be lifted and filled up, and every mountain and hill shall be made low; and the crooked and uneven shall be made straight and level, and the rough places a plain. And the glory (majesty and splendor) of the Lord shall be revealed. . . .
He laid [His] hands on her, and instantly she was made straight, and she recognized and thanked and praised God.

Isaiah 40:4-5; Luke 13:13 AMPC

Sometimes problems, losses, and worries can feel so heavy it's hard to stand up straight, to turn your gaze up to God. So you end up looking down, putting one tentative foot in front of the other, hoping nothing else trips you up.

When Jesus was teaching in the synagogue on the Sabbath, He saw a pitiful woman. For eighteen years, she'd been "bent completely forward and utterly unable to straighten herself up or to look upward" (Luke 13:11 AMPC). Jesus immediately called her over to Him, saying, "Woman, you are released from your infirmity!" (Luke 13:12 AMPC). When He put His hands on her, "instantly she was made straight, and she recognized and thanked and praised God" (Luke 13:13 AMPC).

While the once-crooked woman praised God, the synagogue leader was angry—because Jesus healed her on the Sabbath. So he told the congregants they should come on the other six days to be healed, not on a Sabbath day. Jesus, attempting to straighten *him* out, asked, "Don't

you untie your ox or your donkey from its stall on the Sabbath and lead it out for water?" (Luke 13:15 NLT). If so, "Ought not this woman, a daughter of Abraham, whom Satan has kept bound for eighteen years, be loosed from this bond on the Sabbath day?" (Luke 13:16 AMPC).

Problems, losses, and worries can, at times, seem overwhelming. The remedy lies in seeking God. Keep going to church, praying, asking Him to transform your mind. And don't assume that every thought you have is true. Some are directly planted by Satan, the Father of lies, who hopes to bind you up for years, even a lifetime, with untruths.

Today, seek God and His truths. Allow your faith to override falsehoods. Then let those lies, problems, and worries roll off your back. Commit them to God, knowing He will then make both you and your paths straight!

I don't want untruths to rule over me, Lord. So I'm turning all my thoughts over to You. Show me Your truths, Lord, as I look up and praise You! Amen.

Jesus makes my crooked paths—and thoughts—straight!

Making the Connection

*When the cool evening breezes were blowing, the man and his
wife heard the LORD God walking about in the garden.
So they hid from the LORD God. . . . Then the LORD
God called to the man, "Where are you?" . . .
Humble yourselves before God. . . . Come close
to God, and God will come close to you.*

GENESIS 3:8-9; JAMES 4:7-8 NLT

We're all looking for connection, our arms outstretched, longing to make
contact with another being—whether it be human, animal, or supernatural.
Yet sometimes our arms may fall limp at our sides. Or we may just turn
away. Perhaps, having been burned before, we're thinking, *Why should
I reach out? Why be ignored, abused, rebuffed, abandoned, attacked, or
refused all over again?* Maybe we don't attempt to reach out because
we're hiding, disappointed with ourselves, ashamed of something we've
said or done. At this point, our thoughts may turn darker: *Why put myself
on the line? No one would want me anyway—not even God. I can barely
stand myself!*

Yet God wants us to do what He designed us to do: connect. To love
each other and ourselves. To reach out to all people—no matter their race,
color, nationality, sex, religion, social status, job, or political opinion. Even
more importantly, God wants us to connect to Him.

In the beginning, God spent time with Adam and Eve in the Garden

of Eden. Then one day, after they'd disobeyed Him, they hid, fearing His reaction. Yet even then, God tried to make contact with His children, asking, "Where are you?"

Today, consider what ideas, preconceptions, or self-talk keep you from opening up to and connecting with others. Then consider what thoughts are preventing you from snuggling up close to God. If it's a misdeed, confess it. Ask for His forgiveness. Remember, He's already watching for you, awaiting your arrival, arms spread wide open (Luke 15:20). If you're not connecting because you feel distant from God, remember that if you draw near to Him, He will draw near to you.

Lord, I need some new thoughts, new ideas, new courage to approaching another being. To really put myself out there to help someone else. Show me whom You'd have me connect to. In Jesus' name, amen.

As I come near to God and others, they will come near to me.

Until Storms Pass

*My soul takes refuge and finds shelter and confidence in You; yes,
in the shadow of Your wings will I take refuge and be confident
until calamities and destructive storms are passed. . . .*
*"How often I have wanted to gather your children together as a
hen protects her chicks beneath her wings, but you wouldn't let me."*
PSALM 57:1 AMPC; MATTHEW 23:37 NLT

The book of Psalms contains various records of people's struggles, thoughts, fears, situations, joys, prayers, pleadings, praises, dreams, failures, and victories. Although their words were penned years ago, today's readers can easily relate to them.

Psalm 57 is "a record of memorable thoughts of David when he fled from Saul in the cave" (AMPC). It reads like a journal entry or prayer diary, enlightening readers as to what went through David's mind while he was on the run from a murderous king in 1005 BC.

What's interesting is that, although you might not have a king coming after you, some of David's thoughts may be ones you yourself have entertained from time to time. Perhaps you have wanted to run and hide. Like David, your heart may race and your breath come quickly—but unlike David, there may be no actual physical danger. Yet your thoughts have led you to a place where your body is reacting *as if* someone (or something) is physically chasing you down.

When your fight-flight-freeze response has kicked in without the

physical reality to back it up, you need to replace your anxious thoughts with soothing and empowering words like David's. To get deep into prayer, knowing you have a mighty God looking out for you. It's in Him your soul can find the refuge of God's protective power. Under the shelter of Jesus' wings, you'll find the chance to catch your breath, settle down, and regain your strength. Then, once the storm has passed, when you're calm, cool, and collected, you can face the world again, stronger than ever before.

When your thoughts, fears, and life events take you where you didn't expect or want to go, seek out God. Allow Him to give you the shelter, peace, and rest your soul craves. In so doing, your thoughts will realign with His, leaving you ready to stand tall once more, in Him.

Beneath Your protective wings, Lord, I find shelter. Confident in You and Your power, I regain my strength and energy. I come away transformed in thought and soul. Amen.

In God I take refuge till the storms pass.

Positively Persuaded

I will cry to God Most High, Who performs on my behalf and rewards me [Who brings to pass His purposes for me and surely completes them]! He will send from heaven and save me. . . .
I know (perceive, have knowledge of, and am acquainted with) Him Whom I have believed (adhered to and trusted in and relied on), and I am [positively] persuaded that He is able to guard and keep that which has been entrusted to me and which I have committed [to Him].

PSALM 57:2-3; 2 TIMOTHY 1:12 AMPC

You thought God had a plan. And that you were on board. But things did not at all work out like you expected. Next thing you know, you're thinking God isn't thinking straight. Or that you got the wrong message. Perhaps you didn't do your part right, and so the entire design unraveled. Or maybe someone else messed things up. If he or she hadn't done this or that, everything would still be on target.

And so here you stand. Beginning to doubt what you thought God's plan for you was. Maybe you're starting to think God doesn't keep His word, His promises. This is the beginning of a very slippery slope, my friend.

David went through a lot before he became king of Israel. Even after he was anointed (by God through the prophet Samuel) to take over for King Saul, David was *still* being chased down by him. At one point, Saul threw spears at him, aiming to kill. Then, once David did become king,

his own son tried to dethrone him.

The point is, life can be hard. Even when you're walking where God wants you to walk, doing what He would have you do. Even then you may suffer losses and heartaches, betrayals, and upsets. But take heart. God is with you. He keeps His promises. He *will* make "good on his word" (Psalm 57:3 MSG). So just trust Him. Be positively persuaded in your heart and mind that God is working things out, just as He's planned, for your welfare and His glory.

I know You have a plan for me, Lord, and that You'll bring it to a successful conclusion someday. So I am resolved to let any doubts fall away as I trust in You and Your Word and plan for me. In Jesus' name I pray, amen.

I am positively persuaded God will bring His plan for me to fruition.

Open-Eyed

Elisha prayed, Lord, I pray You, open his eyes that he may see.
And the Lord opened the young man's eyes, and he saw,
and behold, the mountain was full of horses and
chariots of fire round about Elisha. . . .
[Jesus] took the bread and blessed it. Then he broke it
and gave it to them. Suddenly, their eyes were opened,
and they recognized him. And at that moment he disappeared!
2 KINGS 6:17 AMPC; LUKE 24:30-31 NLT

When your thoughts are focused on the obstacles and challenges surrounding you, your fears tend to take center stage. But when you set your sights on the God whom no foe can conquer, suddenly you see things with God's perspective, and faith reigns once more!

The king of Syria was trying, somewhat relentlessly, to attack different towns in Israel. But God, through the prophet Elisha, kept giving the enemy's strategy to the king of Israel, allowing him to move troops where needed to defend God's people.

So the king of Syria decided to go after Elisha in Dothan. He sent horses and chariots to encircle the city under the cover of night. At daybreak, Elisha's servant saw they were surrounded. Full of fear, he said, "Oh, master! What shall we do?" (2 Kings 6:15 MSG).

Elisha told him not to be afraid, that those who were with them were more than those who were with their enemy. Then he prayed that God

would open his servant's eyes so that he could see. "So the LORD opened the eyes of the young man, and he saw, and behold, the mountain was full of horses and chariots of fire all around Elisha" (2 Kings 6:17 ESV).

As the Syrians came down the mountain, Elisha then prayed for God to strike them blind. And God did! Battle over!

God wants you to see things from His perspective—with the eyes of faith. To know that He will protect and provide for you. For when you trust in God, no matter how things seem, your vision is expanded and limitless. Just like God's!

So often, Lord, I find that my fears obscure my vision. Work on me, Lord. Transform my fears to faith. Open my eyes so I can see things from Your unlimited perspective—and in so doing, gain Your everlasting peace. Amen.

In trusting God, I gain new insights, seeing things from His unlimited perspective.

Happy Thoughts

*A happy heart is good medicine and a cheerful mind
works healing, but a broken spirit dries up the bones....
Keep your minds thinking about whatever is true, whatever is
respected, whatever is right, whatever is pure, whatever can be
loved, and whatever is well thought of. If there is anything
good and worth giving thanks for, think about these things.*

PROVERBS 17:22 AMPC; PHILIPPIANS 4:8 NLV

On March 6, 2019, the Associated Press published a short article with the heading, " 'Happy Thoughts' Helped Lost California Girls Survive Ordeal." It went on to say that for almost two days, two sisters, ages five and eight, were lost in a dense forest in Northern California. But they made it through two extremely cold nights by huddling together under a tree branch and a huckleberry bush and by thinking "happy thoughts," words the older sister used to encourage her tearful sibling.

God knows His good words can help you survive, no matter where you go or how lost you might get. But it's up to you to *choose* to think those cheerful thoughts.

Thoughts of doom and gloom can definitely leave you depressed, if not sobbing in your pillow in the dark, cold, and long hours of the night. Negative thinking will also sap your strength, leaving you even more vulnerable to the lies of the evil one.

Fortunately, God provides you with a remedy to the situation. He

tells you to fix your thoughts on good things. To fill every nook and cranny of your mind with things that are true, noble, and worthy of praise. The best, not the worst. The lovely, not the ugly.

That also means taking great care in what you watch and listen to. As far as what you should read, God's Word is highly recommended. Before you begin your day, find an encouraging word from God that you can go think about, memorize, or meditate on throughout your day. At the end of the day, preferably right before bed, write down at least three things you're grateful for. Include specifics. Thank God for them. Then revisit your morning verse. And fall asleep, with its words filling your mind and heart with encouragement and joy.

Lord, today I choose to think happy thoughts. To bolster my heart by thinking of what is good, not bad. So lead me to a verse that would uplift my spirit, as I live in You.

As I fill my mind with happy thoughts, I find God's peace.

Continue to Hope

[Job's] wife said to him, "Do you still hold on to your faith? Curse God and die!" But he said to her. . . "Should we receive good from God and not receive trouble?" In all this Job did not sin with his lips. . . . In your hearts honor Christ the Lord as holy, always being prepared to make a defense to anyone who asks you for a reason for the hope that is in you; yet do it with gentleness and respect.

JOB 2:9-10 NLV; 1 PETER 3:15 ESV

Just when you're at your lowest, trying to keep it together, someone may come along and say a discouraging word. It happens to the best of us. And it happened to Job.

Unbeknownst to Job, Satan had gone before God, asking if he could test his faith. For he believed the only reason Job was faithful to God was because he had a great life. The evil one's desire was to make life so bad for Job that he would curse God and die (Job 1:11; 2:4). So God told Satan he could mess with Job—but he couldn't kill him.

Satan began testing Job's faith by taking everything from Job except his wife and his health. Still Job remained faithful, saying, "The Lord gives and takes away. Praise God's name" (Job 1:21, paraphrased). Satan's second faith-breaking attempt was to inflict painful sores on Job's body, from head to toe.

While Job sat in ashes, scraping his sores with a broken piece of pottery, his wife asked if he was still holding on to his faith, advising him

to "curse God and die!" But Job refused, saying, "Should we receive good from God and not receive trouble?"

Chances are your faith will be tested. Bad things do happen to good people. And while you're down in the dumps, pre-Christians may ask you questions like, "Where's your God now?" That's when you need to hold on to your faith *and* your hope and godly thoughts. To respond to the questions of nonbelievers with gentleness and respect. To remember that God is in charge of everything—including your life. That He loves you, has a plan for you. That somehow, no matter how bad things look, God *will* work things out for your good.

Just continue to hope.

Lord, I'm not sure why bad things sometimes happen. But I will continue to have faith and hope in You. That somehow You will work things out for my good! Amen.

In trials, my faith and hope will bring me through.

A Faith Fixation

The thing which I greatly fear comes upon me, and that of which I am afraid befalls me. I was not or am not at ease, nor had I or have I rest, nor was I or am I quiet, yet trouble came and still comes [upon me]. . . . Do not fret or have any anxiety about anything, but in every circumstance and in everything, by prayer and petition (definite requests), with thanksgiving, continue to make your wants known to God. And God's peace. . .shall garrison and mount guard over your hearts and minds in Christ Jesus.

Job 3:25-26; Philippians 4:6-7 ampc

Job was "blameless and upright" (Job 1:1 AMPC), a man who truly feared God. And he had everything—a wealth of money, animals, servants, and family members. Yet still he had fears.

Job's greatest fear was that his children would misstep, disown God in their hearts. So every time all the kids got together at one of their homes for a birthday feast, the next day Job would offer sacrifices for them.

Yet still, there came a day when all Job had was wiped out, including his children. He had nothing left but his health. Then that too was taken.

At the time, Job didn't know God was letting Satan test him. He also didn't know that in the end God would not just restore but give Job more than he'd had in the beginning.

We too don't know why bad things sometimes happen to good people. But there's one thing we do know: God doesn't want you to be fixated

on your fears. For if you're totally focused on the things you dread will happen, chances are you're not going to God and praying about them. And if you're not praying about them, you're limiting God's power to help you.

Jesus made it clear that you're not to worry about anything but to bring all your anxieties and fears to God. Lay them at His feet. Ask for His help. For as you do so, your fears are in God's hands and your mind is fixed on Him not what may or may not happen.

Today, take whatever you dread may happen to God. Mindfully focus on your faith instead of your fears. Then, you'll have God's peace.

Lord, I want that tranquil soul You promise. So today, I'm bringing You all my fears, all my what-ifs, knowing that as I do so, You'll fill me with the peace I desire. In Jesus' name, amen.

As I give God my fears, I gain His peace.

Great Expectations

The Lord [earnestly] waits [expecting, looking, and longing] to be
gracious to you. . .and show loving-kindness to you. . . . Blessed (happy,
fortunate, to be envied) are all those who [earnestly] wait for
Him, who expect and look and long for Him [for His victory,
His favor, His love, His peace, His joy, and His
matchless, unbroken companionship]! . . .
He who believes in Him. . .shall not be put to
shame nor be disappointed in his expectations.
ISAIAH 30:18; ROMANS 9:33 AMPC

Disciples Peter and John were heading to the temple in Jerusalem at about three in the afternoon. Outside one of the gates, they came across a man who'd been lame since birth. There he would be carried, then laid down so he could beg for alms, charitable gifts, from temple goers.

When Peter and John came across him as they were entering the temple, he asked them for a handout. Both the apostles stared at him. Peter said, "Look at us" (Acts 3:4 AMPC). "And [the man] paid attention to them, expecting that he was going to get something from them" (Acts 3:5 AMPC). Peter said, "I don't have any money. But I do have something I can give you." He then called down the power of Jesus Christ, and said, "Walk!" As he pulled up the man, the beggar's feet and ankles were healed instantly! He stood, walked, and then began jumping around, leaping his way into the temple and praising God. This lame beggar expected

money but received so much more!

God often moves beyond your expectations, giving you something even better or larger, going beyond what you had ever hoped or desired. So while you're waiting for God to work in your life, don't give in to negative thoughts. Don't begin thinking you've asked for too much. Don't give up praying or waiting, imagining God either hasn't heard or will not answer your prayers.

Instead, pray big. Recognize, believe that God is longing to be kind to and show His love for you in a miraculous way. Find joy in the fact that as you wait for Him, He's gearing up to bless you, in His time. So keep your expectations high. And keep your eye out for His victory, favor, love, peace, joy, and "matchless, unbroken companionship."

I'm looking to You, Lord, to go beyond
what I expect or imagine! Amen!

God blesses me beyond my expectations!

Go with Confidence

*"The Lord has filled Bezalel with the Spirit of God, giving him
great wisdom, ability, and expertise in all kinds of crafts." . . .
May the God of peace. . .equip you with all you need for doing
his will. May he produce in you, through the power of Jesus
Christ, every good thing that is pleasing to him.*

EXODUS 35:31; HEBREWS 13:20-21 NLT

When God calls you to do something, you may wish you were as brave as someone like Moses. Yet even that great man wasn't always so confident or courageous.

When God came to Moses, telling him to lead His people out of Egypt, Moses said, "But why me? What makes you think that I could. . . ?" (Exodus 3:11 MSG). Moses obviously thought he was unworthy. At the same time, he probably feared going back to Egypt. Last time he was there he'd killed a man. So God reassured him: "No worries. I'll be with you."

Moses' next excuse: "What if people ask me who sent me? What do I say?" Moses felt uncomfortable being put in a situation where he didn't have all the answers. But God had them. He told Moses to tell them the "I-Am sent me" (Exodus 3:14 MSG).

Moses' third excuse: "What if they don't believe me?" A valid fear for anyone, right? For if people don't believe you, they may react somewhat threateningly. So God said He'd provide Moses with a staff through which miracles can be wrought. That should be proof enough that God's with him.

Next, Moses told God he wasn't good with words. So God said He'd tell him what to say. Lastly, when Moses begged for God to send someone else, his holy Father finally got angry. Yet He continued to equip Moses with everything he needed, including his brother and now spokesperson, Aaron. In the end, Moses successfully freed God's people, leading them to the Promised Land.

When God calls you, don't let your thoughts of unworthiness, lack, what-ifs, or fears crowd out your God-given confidence and courage. Be assured He will not just be with you but will support, equip, and empower you, ensuring a successful mission.

So often, Lord, my fears and negative thoughts give me lead feet. Help me remember that You have promised to be with me and equip me with all I need to successfully answer Your call. Amen.

God equips me with everything I could possibly need to answer His call!

Do-Badders vs. Do-Gooders

Don't worry about the wicked or envy those who do wrong.
For like grass, they soon fade away.... Trust in the LORD and
do good. Then you will live safely in the land and prosper....
"Turn away from evil and do good.... The eyes of the LORD watch
over those who do right, and his ears are open to their prayers.
But the LORD turns his face against those who do evil."
PSALM 37:1-3; 1 PETER 3:11-12 NLT

Some people are not just unkind but evil. Yet many are also successful, at least in how this world defines *success*. They have money, great careers, travel everywhere, and seem so happy. And there you are, a do-gooder, just trying to eke by. Compared to them, your work, home, and family life seem humdrum.

Some nights, as you stumble into bed—so that you can wake up and do it all over again—you may begin to wonder if you're leading the right kind of life. *Why not start cutting corners at work? No one will ever know—and you'll be able to finally have enough money to get what you want*, whispers a voice from the darkness. Don't believe it!

God wants you to forget about the people who do all the wrong things for all the wrong reasons. It's you and your prayers He listens to, rewarding you with His kind of safety, prosperity, and eternal life. All you need to do is trust Him!

Remember Jezebel? At one point, this evil queen must've thought

she had it all! More power and riches than she could count. But God was against her. And He got her in the end.

After painting her face, Queen Jezebel stuck her head out a window and saw Jehu. He told the eunuchs with her to throw her out that window. And they did! Jehu then drove over her with his horses. When they went to bury her, all that was left were her "skull, feet, and palms of her hands" (2 Kings 9:35 AMPC).

Don't let your admiration for the rich nor your frustration with your worldly means lead you down the wrong road. Turn away from the do-badders and continue doing good. Look to God for all you need and desire. He's open to working with you so you can prosper—in Him!

Keep from my mind worries about rich do-badders, Lord. I'm keeping my eyes on You, knowing You're keeping Your eyes on me! Amen.

I trust God to take care of do-badders.

Rising Prayers

He will surely be gracious to you at the sound of your cry; when He
hears it, He will answer you. . . . And your ears will hear a word
behind you, saying, This is the way; walk in it, when you
turn to the right hand and when you turn to the left. . . .
There was silence for about half an hour in heaven. . . .
And the smoke of the incense (the perfume) arose in
the presence of God, with the prayers of the people
of God (the saints), from the hand of the angel.
ISAIAH 30:19, 21; REVELATION 8:1, 4 AMPC

You have a decision to make. So you make a list of pros and cons, gains and pains. Then you might ask friends, a spouse, coworkers, and relatives what they think. After you weigh all that analysis and advice, you check within, trying to determine your own "gut" feeling. But still you feel unsure. Everyone seems to have different advice. Even your intuition and thoughts seem to contradict each other. What's a woman to do? Consult God and His Word.

The prophet Isaiah tells you very plainly that when you cry out to God for help, He will hear your prayer—and answer it!

But how do you step away from the anxiety, quiet the what-ifs, and clear the thoughts rampaging within so that you can hear God's voice? You begin by sitting quietly before the Lord. Amid the silence, you breathe deeply, settling yourself physically, mentally, and emotionally. Allow

your thoughts to drift in and out. Then focus on some calming scripture, imagining God speaking into your life, saying something like, "Let be and be still, and know. . .that I am God" (Psalm 46:10 AMPC).

Once you have calmed your heart, soul, spirit, body, and mind, enter God's presence more deeply. Know that He's listening, hearing you. That your prayer has risen up and is now in His presence. Imagine that yours is the only prayer He hears in this moment. Know that He will answer by any means available. Perhaps it will be through His Word, a fellow human, or circumstances.

The point is to keep calm, knowing God is working on your behalf and will guide you. He will answer your prayer—if your mind, heart, ears, and spirit are open.

I don't know what to do, where to go, Lord. So I'm coming to You. Guide me step-by-step, into Your wisdom. Amen.

God hears my prayer and guides me to His wisdom.

A Blessed Blessing

The one who blesses others is abundantly
blessed; those who help others are helped. . . .
This most generous God. . .is more than extravagant with you.
He gives you something you can. . .give away, which grows into full-
formed lives, robust in God, wealthy in every way, so that you can be
generous in every way, producing with us great praise to God.
PROVERBS 11:25; 2 CORINTHIANS 9:10-11 MSG

When you're down in the dumps, tired of your problems, stressed out over the day's to-do list, or looking to find a way out of the woe-is-me thought cycle, stop. Get out of your own mind's meanderings by doing something nice for someone else.

God's Word tells you that if you bless someone, you yourself will be blessed. If you help someone, you yourself will be helped. It's a spiritual law!

Thinking you're not blessed right now, in this moment? Perhaps it's time to take stock of your situation. To understand, recognize, and believe God has blessed you "with every spiritual blessing in the heavenly realms" because you're one with Christ (Ephesian 1:3 NLT). So before going any further, take a moment to write down all the things you have, all the things going right in your life. Then, get out there and be a blessing to someone else. For as soon as you step out of your life and into someone else's, you'll find your way back to the joy of life!

So what can you do, how can you bless someone else? Ask God to open your eyes, to show you where He wants you to go, whose life He wants you to touch. Just in that asking, comes your first blessing, as you realize your mind is no longer on yourself but on God and others. Then step out into the world, waiting for God to provide an opportunity to bless.

Perhaps God will lead you to a neighbor, a friend, a family member, or a complete stranger. A blessing could simply be the gift of your smile. Maybe it'll be more physical, such as opening a door, carrying groceries, walking a dog, or raking leaves. Perhaps you'll feel called to reach out with a word of encouragement via email, text, or a handwritten letter.

It doesn't matter how or where or who you bless. Simply bless. And you too will be blessed.

Show me whom I can joyfully bless and help,
Lord, as You have blessed and helped me. Amen.

As I bless others, I myself find blessings.

Life's Turnings

Rouse Yourself [O Lord] to meet and help me, and see! . . .
O my Strength, I will watch and give heed to You and sing
praises; for God is my Defense (my Protector and High Tower).
My God in His mercy and steadfast love will meet me. . . .
She turned around and saw Jesus standing, but she did not know
that it was Jesus. Jesus said to her, "Woman, why are
you weeping? Whom are you seeking?"
PSALM 59:4, 9-10 AMPC; JOHN 20:14-15 ESV

Imagine you're Mary Magdalene. Your Friend, Teacher, Master, and Defender has been killed. In tears and confusion, you head out early in the morning, walking to His tomb. To your horror and surprise, you see the stone has been rolled away. They've taken your Beloved—and you don't know where! So you run to Peter and John, telling them what's happened. They run back with you, see the tomb empty. Nothing is left of their Savior but what His body had been wrapped in.

Your friends see all this and go back home. Yet you remain, weeping. You stoop down to look into the tomb, wanting to see things for yourself. Two angels are sitting there, where your Friend had once lain. They ask why you're crying. You say, "Because they've taken my Friend's body, and I know not where."

You turn and see a Man standing before you. He asks why you're crying. Thinking He's just the gardener, you say, "Sir, if you have carried

him away, tell me where you have laid him, and I will take him away" (John 20:15 ESV). And then He says your name. You turn once more and see Jesus. You fall to the ground, clutching His feet, never wanting to release Him. But He commands you to let go and tell others. Now calm, at peace, you turn to go, carrying the good news with you.

Amid your griefs and troubles, Jesus will rouse Himself and meet with you. No matter which way you turn, where your path may lead, what you may suffer, as you seek out and pray to God—your Defense, Protector, and High Tower—He will meet you.

Woman, why are you troubled? Whom are you seeking? Turn and see your Beloved Jesus, waiting to help you, meet you, see you.

Meet with me, Jesus. I long for Your presence, Your touch, Your protection. In Your name I pray, amen.

Jesus meets me where and when I seek Him.

Standing Firm

*I will sing of Your mighty strength and power; yes, I will sing aloud
of Your mercy and loving-kindness in the morning; for You have been
to me a defense (a fortress and a high tower) and a refuge. . . .
Put on God's complete armor, that you may be able to resist and
stand your ground on the evil day [of danger], and, having done
all [the crisis demands], to stand [firmly in your place].*
PSALM 59:16; EPHESIANS 6:13 AMPC

When you feel you're not strong enough to fight off all the negative
thoughts and powers coming against you, you have no need to fear or
worry. You've got God on your side. And, as always, He's more than ready
to not just protect you but equip you to meet whatever comes.

God knows that if you get into Him and His Word before you get
into your day, you'll have all the spiritual gear you need to defend
yourself. It begins by covering yourself in God's truth, not the random
thoughts in your own mind, things that seem like truth but may not be.
Next, protect yourself by being right with God. Slip your feet into God's
peace so you can stand tall. Most of all, cover yourself in faith, leaving
all doubts in the hamper. That's how you'll be able to extinguish any
fiery darts the devil shoots your way. Next, cover your head with the
fact that Jesus has saved you. Then take up your one and only weapon,
"the sword of the Spirit which is the Word of God" (Ephesians 6:17 NLV),
giving you all the power you need to skewer the mistruths and lies o

122

others. And above all, pray. All. . .the. . .time.

Now that you're all geared up, you're a defender, not a victim. You're a strong woman in the Lord. No earthly spirit can conquer you, because you have the heavenly Spirit within and over you, leading you, guiding you.

Go in this godly strength and power, knowing that you can resist whatever comes. You can do what you can amid any crisis. Then, having done all you can, you can firmly stand your ground.

In God, you are a woman of power. Of God, you are protected by the Master and Creator of the universe. He is on your side. So fear nothing. Simply trust your Lord and Master—and stand.

Of God's mighty strength and power, I sing! Amen.

God empowers me to stand firmly in His strength.

Slow to Anger

Stop being angry! Turn from your rage!
Do not lose your temper—it only leads to harm. . . .
You must all be quick to listen, slow to speak, and slow to
get angry. Human anger does not produce
the righteousness God desires.

PSALM 37:8; JAMES 1:19-20 NLT

Anger cannot only harm others but yourself. For Jesus says anyone angry with a brother or sister is the same as a murderer and subject to the same punishment. He goes even further, saying, "Words kill" (Matthew 5:22 MSG)!

Those are some pretty strong words, yet they're true. So how does one stay clear of anger? It all begins with your thoughts.

Wrong thoughts typically lead to wrong actions. Take Cain. Both he and his brother Abel made an offering to God. Cain presented some of his harvest to God. But Abel gave God the best of his lambs. God accepted Abel's offering but not Cain's. This led Cain to think God liked Abel better than He liked him. So in his anger, Cain killed Abel, a move which got Cain banished from God's presence. (See Genesis 4.)

Take Moses. God told him to speak to a rock and it would yield up water. But Moses, angry with the complaints of God's people, most likely decided, "I'll show these people. I'll fix this problem and then they'll shut up." So he struck the rock twice. That lack of faith, of not leaving the situation and his own frustration in God's hands, kept Moses from

entering the Promised Land. (See Numbers 20.)

Then there was the hapless Haman. His anger, around the fact that Mordecai the Jew wouldn't bow to him (Esther 3:5), led Haman to think wrong thoughts which then led him to take drastic measures. First, he had the king sign a decree to annihilate the Jews. Then he built gallows on which he intended Mordecai would be hung. But God had other plans. And it was Haman himself who ended up hanged.

When anger arises, stop. Examine your thoughts that led you to this point. Check and see if you're taking things too personally, have wrong expectations, or are ignoring the brighter side of a situation. Then turn your thoughts over to God, asking Him to exchange yours with His. And begin training yourself to be "quick to listen, slow to speak, and slow to get angry" (James 1:19 NLT).

Help me curb my anger, Lord,
so that I stay right with others—and You! Amen.

With God's help, I can rein in anger and speak words of peace.

God's Arm

O Lord, be gracious to us; we have waited [expectantly] for You.
Be the arm [of Your servants—their strength and defense]
every morning, our salvation in the time of trouble. . . .
Be alert and on your guard; stand firm in your faith. . . .
Be courageous; grow in strength!
ISAIAH 33:2; 1 CORINTHIANS 16:13 AMPC

When life gets really hard, your thoughts can lead you in the wrong direction. You may begin saying to yourself, "I just can't go on anymore. I have no more hope. I'm too tired, too discouraged to even lift my head." These ideas can lead you down an even darker path, one that might lead you to seek help from something or someone other than God.

Yet God warns His people about seeking aid from other camps: "Woe to those who go down to Egypt for help, who rely on horses and trust in chariots because they are many and in horsemen because they are very strong, but they look not to the Holy One of Israel, nor seek and consult the Lord!" (Isaiah 31:1 AMPC). Back in the prophet Isaiah's day, the people of Judah could see the many horses and the strength of the riders. They could find a reason to trust them. But they couldn't seem to come up with a reason to trust God.

God wants you to seek help from Him only. Not to reach out to men and women who seem strong, to trust in them more than your Lord. Instead, God wants you to wait on Him. To ask Him only to be your

strength, support, and defense every morning. Your place of safety in times of trouble. That is where you'll get the energy you need to not just carry on but to do what needs to be done. For God has proven, time and time again, that *He* is the only One who can truly save you—from weakness, from yourself.

The apostle Paul, writer of 1 Corinthians, agrees. When you're walking a life of faith, following Jesus, he strongly advises you to be alert. To stand your ground, firm in your faith. To keep on trusting your creator. To be brave. And to grow in strength and power. As you do so, God will be there. To catch you, to save you, to bring you to victory!

Lord, be my strength and my defense every morning,
as I move forward in Your power. Amen.

God is my strength and protection every morning!

A Rock-Solid Retreat

My people shall dwell in a peaceable habitation,
in safe dwellings, and in quiet resting-places. . . .
And the woman [herself] fled into the desert (wilderness),
where she has a retreat prepared [for her] by God,
in which she is to be fed and kept safe. . . .
When my heart is overwhelmed and fainting; lead me
to the rock that is higher than I. . . . For You have been
a shelter and a refuge for me, a strong tower.

ISAIAH 32:18; REVELATION 12:6; PSALM 61:2-3 AMPC

One of the ways God can transform you is through His Word. But a surface reading won't do. To dig deeper into what God may be saying to you, consider reading one chapter each in the Old Testament, the New Testament, and Psalms every day. Underline the verses that strike a chord deep within. Record them in a journal, meditate on them, pray about them. And you might be amazed at what you discover!

Consider the verses in today's reading. The first verse comes from the Lord, speaking through the prophet Isaiah. In the proceeding chapters, God asked His people to trust in Him. He's promised them that a Messiah and His Spirit will make things right. In Isaiah 32:18, God says His trusting people will live in a peaceful place, where things are safe and quiet. A place where they can rest and be refueled in Him.

The next verses from Revelation concern a woman who, having just

given birth to a child (Revelation 12:5), is in a weakened state. Realizing her vulnerability, she runs into the desert. There God has prepared a retreat for her, one in which she'll be nourished and kept safe.

In the last verses, you discover the thoughts of a psalmist whose heart is overwhelmed and faint. He cries out to God, asking Him to lead him to a rock that is higher than he. A rock (like Christ) on which he will feel sheltered, safe, secure.

All three passages are a message to you from God. He wants you to know that whenever you're overwhelmed—in thought, word, or deed—He has a place prepared for you. A place where you can be kept safe, nourished, and sheltered, and bask in His peace. Thoughtfully seek that place in God's presence today.

Thank You for Your Word and the shelter it provides me, Lord. Lead me to Your quiet resting place. Amen.

In God I find peace, rest, and safety.

First Thing

Fear not [there is nothing to fear], for I am with you; do not look around you in terror and be dismayed, for I am your God. I will strengthen and harden you to difficulties, yes, I will help you; yes, I will hold you up and retain you with My [victorious] right hand of rightness and justice. . . .
"So don't worry about these things, saying, 'What will we eat? What will we drink? . . .' These things dominate the thoughts of unbelievers, but your heavenly Father already knows all your needs. Seek the Kingdom of God above all else, and live righteously, and he will give you everything you need."
Isaiah 41:10 ampc; Matthew 6:31-33 nlt

When you're living paycheck to paycheck, it can be difficult not to worry or be filled with fear. Because one big hospital bill, car repair, tornado, flood, or tax payment can wipe you out. Younger people may have it even harder, as they struggle to pay off college loans, finance a car, or save up for a wedding or dream home. The current reality is that many people, except a privileged few, are stressed because of money issues. And heaven only knows when this huge disparity in income will become a thing of the past.

So what does God's daughter do in the meantime? The Word gives clear direction. First, God says you're not to fear. He, your all-powerful and loving God, is walking with you. He doesn't want you looking around

in terror, being dismayed, discouraged, fearful, fretful, or fitfully wringing your hands. God is going to strengthen you during these difficult times—*and* help you! He'll hold you up, keep you on your feet.

Second, don't worry about your wants and needs. Those things are *constantly* on the minds of *pre*-Christians—but shouldn't be on yours. Because your God already knows your needs.

Third, instead of fearing or worrying, "Steep your life in God-reality, God-initiative, God-provisions. . . . You'll find all your everyday human concerns will be met" (Matthew 6:33 MSG). That means to put worry on the back burner and God on the front burner. Make seeking Him out and living a right life your number one priority, and everything else will fall into place!

I'm tired of worrying about money, Lord, and what the lack of it may mean. Instead, I'm seeking You, knowing You'll provide all I need! Amen.

As I seek God, He provides for me in every way.

Regardless!

*All the days of the desponding and afflicted are made evil
[by anxious thoughts and forebodings], but he who has a glad
heart has a continual feast [regardless of circumstances]. . . .
Be happy [in your faith] and rejoice and be glad-hearted
continually (always). . .thank [God] in everything [no matter
what the circumstances may be, be thankful and give thanks].*
PROVERBS 15:15; 1 THESSALONIANS 5:16-18 AMPC

Phineas and his brother Hophni were priests, just like their father Eli. But they weren't the best of priests—at all. The Bible describes them as "worthless; they did not know or regard the Lord" (1 Samuel 2:12 AMPC). They did shoddy work at the temple and slept with the servants there (1 Samuel 2:13-17, 22).

Then one day Phineas and Hophni, on the advice of Israel's elders, carried the ark of God into battle against the Philistines, treating the ark as a sort of good luck symbol, a sacred object. At first the Philistines were afraid. But once they gathered up their courage, they won the battle, killed the priests, and captured the ark!

Hearing this bad news, Eli fell over, broke his neck, and died. Hearing the ark had been captured, and her husband, brother-in-law, and father-in-law were dead, Phineas's pregnant wife went into labor and delivered a child. To comfort and cheer her, her midwives said, "Don't be afraid. You have born a son!" But she neither answered nor paid attention. Just

before she died, she named her son Ichabod, which means, "The glory has departed from Israel" (1 Samuel 4:21 ESV), because "the ark of God has been captured" (1 Samuel 4:22 ESV).

Phineas's wife—filled with anxious thoughts and hopelessness, believing more in the ark than God Himself—stands in stark contrast to the faith-filled and hopeful Paul and Silas. Having been thrown in jail, they "were at prayer and singing a robust hymn to God. . . . Then, without warning, a huge earthquake! The jailhouse tottered, every door flew open, all the prisoners were loose" (Acts 16:25-26 MSG).

Regardless of what's happening in your life, do not give in to anxious thoughts, hopelessness, or evil forebodings. Seek God's true presence and find a bright side. Allow your heart to feast on God and His love and protection. Then raise your voice in praise and thanksgiving! And God will rock your world, opening up new opportunities, just for you!

Change up my thoughts, Lord, so I may be happy no matter what's happening in my life. Amen!

In God I find joy—in all circumstances!

Heartfelt Prayer

This people draw near Me with their mouth and honor Me with their
lips but remove their hearts and minds far from Me, and their fear
and reverence for Me are a commandment of men that is learned
by repetition [without any thought as to the meaning]. . . .
When you pray, do not heap up phrases (multiply words, repeating
the same ones over and over) as the Gentiles do, for they think they
will be heard for their much speaking. . . . Pray, therefore, like this:
Our Father Who is in heaven, hallowed (kept holy) be Your name.
Isaiah 29:13; Matthew 6:7, 9 ampc

God loves to have you snuggle up close to Him, whispering prayers that come directly from your heart. What He *doesn't* want is for you to come to Him dragging your feet, your mind and heart not really in the words you speak, giving no real thought to their meaning.

Jesus agrees. He told His followers not to just keep saying the same words over and over again, as if God were a doddering grandpa who was forgetful or partially deaf. Instead, Jesus taught you how to pray by giving you the Lord's Prayer as an example.

Yet think back to the last time you prayed the Lord's Prayer. . . . Was your heart or mind really in it or have you said it so often that it has lost its meaning? If the former is true, that's great. If you fit into the latter category, you may want to slow down when you say it, making sure it comes directly from your heart. Or look at other translations of

the prayer, ones that might breathe new life into your time with God. Here's the Lord's Prayer from *The Message* (Matthew 6:9-13):

> *Our Father in heaven,*
> *Reveal who you are.*
> *Set the world right;*
> *Do what's best—*
> *as above, so below.*
> *Keep us alive with three square meals.*
> *Keep us forgiven with you and forgiving others.*
> *Keep us safe from ourselves and the Devil.*
> *You're in charge!*
> *You can do anything you want!*
> *You're ablaze in beauty!*
> *Yes. Yes. Yes.*

Regardless of the words you use, always remember God doesn't want just your lips to move when you come into His presence. He wants your heart, spirit, soul, and mind to be moved as well.

My moving, heartfelt prayers move God.

Mighty Conqueror

With God's help we will do mighty things. . . .
If God is for us, who [can be] against us? [Who can be our
foe, if God is on our side?] . . . We are more than conquerors
and gain a surpassing victory through Him Who loved us.
PSALM 60:12 NLT; ROMANS 8:31, 37 AMPC

When you think you're powerless, too insignificant to matter, too low on the social or economic scale to make a difference in this world, remember who you are: a daughter of God.

In the day of Judges, before Israel had kings, the prophet Deborah sent for her people's army commander, Barak. She told him God wanted him to lead his army of 10,000 men and defeat the cruel King Jabin of Canaan. His general Sisera had a huge army and 900 iron chariots under his command.

Even though Deborah had told Barak that God would give the enemy into his hand, Barak said he wouldn't go unless Deborah went with him. Deborah replied, "I'll go with you. But understand that with an attitude like that, there'll be no glory in it for you. GOD will use a woman's hand to take care of Sisera" (Judges 4:9 MSG).

With God's help, Barak did rout the enemy army. But Sisera got down from his chariot and fled on foot. He made it to the tent of Jael, the wife of Heber, a metalsmith friendly with Sisera. She invited him in and covered him with a blanket. He asked for water. She gave him milk.

She even agreed to keep his presence in her tent a secret. Then, while Sisera slept, she grabbed a tent peg and a hammer, sneaked up on him, and drove the peg into Sisera's temple, killing him. Later, Deborah sang a victory song, calling Jael the "most blessed among women" (Judges 5:24 NLT).

Hopefully, God will not move you to take such drastic measures as did Jael. But He does want you and all other women to know that with His help, you can do mighty deeds. Even if you're the wife of a common laborer, using whatever you happen to have on hand. With God, you *can* make a difference, be a conqueror, gaining a victory for Him, through Him!

Lord, help me get thoughts like "I can't" out of my head.
For You have told me, your daughter, that with You
by my side, I can be a mighty conqueror! Amen.

With God's help, I can do mighty things!

Your Strong Place

*My soul is quiet and waits for God alone. My hope comes
from Him. He alone is my rock and the One Who saves
me. He is my strong place. I will not be shaken. . . .
"Here's what I want you to do: Find a quiet, secluded place so
you won't be tempted to role-play before God. Just be there as
simply and honestly as you can manage. The focus will shift
from you to God, and you will begin to sense his grace."*

PSALM 62:5-6 NLV; MATTHEW 6:6 MSG

When you first awaken, still a bit drowsy from sleep, you have an amazing
opportunity to get things right in your head before your feet hit the floor.

In the silence of the morning, "Seek out the book of the Lord and
read" (Isaiah 34:16 AMPC). In His Word, in those moments, underline
whatever words, sentences, or passages feed your soul. Then, while all is
truly quiet, inside and out, relax your body and wait for God. Expect Him,
your Rock, Defense, and Fortress, to meet with you. Pour out your heart to
Him (Psalm 62:6). Eagerly listen for Him to speak to you, comforting you,
directing you, guiding you, filling you with His strength, love, and Spirit.

If your thoughts start to wander, talk to your soul, saying, "My soul, wait
only upon God and silently submit to Him; for my hope and expectation
are from Him" (Psalm 62:5 AMPC).

Why do all this? So that you will be geared up (instead of "feared"
up) to meet whatever comes your way. Having met up with God and His

Word in the spiritual world before dipping your toe in the material world, you'll find yourself trusting God, leaning and relying on Him, placing all your confidence in Him, focusing on Him instead of yourself. And because you've put Him first, He'll put you first! And when you finally do arise, nothing will shake you because you've ensconced yourself in the most holy and magnificent of refuges: Your God—a "Rock of unyielding strength and impenetrable hardness" (Psalm 62:7 AMPC).

This morning, before you go anyplace, go in that "strong place." A secluded place. A place where you could be powered up by no one other than the Creator of the universe.

Before I go anywhere or do anything, Lord, I come seeking You and Your Word. My soul is quiet as I wait for You alone. Amen.

With a quiet soul, I seek God. In Him, I will not be shaken.

Riches in God

*If riches increase, set not your heart on them. Once God
has spoken; twice have I heard this: that power belongs to
God, and that to you, O Lord, belongs steadfast love. . . .
People who long to be rich fall into temptation and are trapped by
many foolish and harmful desires that plunge them into ruin and
destruction. For the love of money is the root of all kinds of evil.*
Psalm 62:10-12 esv; 1 Timothy 6:9-10 nlt

In the early days of the church, "all the believers. . .felt that what they owned was not their own, so they shared everything they had" (Acts 4:32 nlt). To ensure everyone had everything they needed, those who had houses or land would sell their property and turn the money over to the apostles to distribute among the less fortunate.

Enter the well-to-do Ananias and his wife, Sapphira, who decided to sell some property. But they colluded together to bring just part of the proceeds to the apostles. They put the rest aside for themselves, yet claimed they were giving up the total amount.

Ananias went alone before the apostles and dropped the money at their feet. But Peter knew right away that Ananias had kept some of the money back for himself. What Peter didn't understand was why. After all, Ananias didn't *have* to turn over all the proceeds. It would've been fine if he'd held some back. Peter told Ananias he hadn't just lied to the Holy Spirit and fellow believers but to God Himself! As soon as he said

this, Ananias fell over dead and his body was dragged away.

About three hours later, Sapphira appeared, not knowing her husband was dead. Peter asked, "Was this the price you and your husband received for your land?" (Acts 5:8 NLT). She said it was. Peter then asked, "How could the two of you even think of conspiring to test the Spirit of the Lord like this?" (Acts 5:9 NLT). And she too fell over dead.

God wants your thoughts focused on who you are (a daughter of God, sister of Jesus, and vessel for the Holy Spirit), not on what you may (or may not) have. Don't set your heart on money or possessions but on God (the ultimate Power and Provider).

Lord, help me remember that You, not money, hold all the power.
To You, not riches, I pledge all my faith and love. Amen.

As I set my heart and mind on God,
I'm provided with all I need.

Persistence

*I. . .cry out for help and put my hope in your words. I stay
awake through the night, thinking about your promise.
In your faithful love, O LORD, hear my cry. . . .
Be. . .cheerfully expectant. Don't quit in
hard times; pray all the harder.*

PSALM 119:147-149 NLT; ROMANS 12:12 MSG

When you're worn down and tired physically, emotionally, and mentally,
it can prove difficult to stay the course. Thoughts like, *This is never going
to work. I may as well give up*, begin to take their toll. That's when you
need to lean in to God, pluck up courage, and persevere.

Jesus told His followers how they should keep on praying, never give
up. He said there was a judge who didn't care about people or fear God.
But this widow kept coming to Him, crying for justice. Her persistence
finally broke down His resistance, and He gave her what she sought.
Jesus asked His listeners, "Will not God make the things that are right
come to His chosen people who cry day and night to Him? . . . I tell you,
He will be quick to help them" (Luke 18:7-8 NLV).

To be persistent in prayer and life, even during times of extreme
hardship, you need to have faith and hang on to your hope that God will
move on your behalf—no matter how things look or seem.

Rizpah, Saul's concubine, had such faith and hope. Her two sons,
as well as five of Saul's grandsons, were hanged on a mountain. For five

months she stayed on that mountain, keeping from the bodies the birds of the air by day and the wild animals by night. When she did manage to get some sleep, it was on a burlap bag she'd spread out on a rock. Eventually, King David, hearing of Rizpah's plight, gathered the remains of Saul, Jonathan, her two sons, and Saul's five grandsons. He had them all "given a decent burial" (2 Samuel 21:14 MSG). Talk about perseverance!

When you're worn down and feel like giving up, remember these two widows. Consider their stories, today's opening scriptures, and the words of Jesus. Tell yourself to be cheerfully expectant. That you will not quit but will pray all the harder.

God, You're the One who gives me the energy, power, and strength to not give in to defeatist thoughts. Hear my prayer as I cry out to You. Replenish my hope, increase my faith, as I persevere in You. Amen.

Through prayer, hope, and faith, I persevere.

Nevertheless

The inhabitants of Jebus said to David, "You will not come in here."
Nevertheless, David took the stronghold of Zion, that is,
the city of David. . . . And David became greater and
greater, for the LORD of hosts was with him. . . .
"Behold, I cast out demons and perform cures today and
tomorrow, and the third day I finish my course. Nevertheless,
I must go on my way today and tomorrow and the day following."
1 CHRONICLES 11:5, 9; LUKE 13:32-33 ESV

So you've got a plan. You think it's great—*and* it seems to meet with God's approval. But then you come up against people who try to dissuade you from your goal. They're doing everything they can to discourage you, mocking you and your efforts, even threatening you. Soon you begin thinking you don't have the courage, resources, smarts, or faith to see things through. This is when you need to go to God. To get it firmly set in your mind that God is with you, helping you.

When David was crowned king of Israel, he and his people went to Jerusalem. The Jebusites living there taunted him, saying, "You'll never get in here! Even the blind and lame could keep you out!" (2 Samuel 5:6 NLT). "*Nevertheless*, David took the stronghold" (1 Chronicles 11:5 ESV, emphasis added)! Renamed the City of David, it became his seat of power!

Thousands of years later, David's descendent Jesus had His own *nevertheless* moment! As He was making His way to Jerusalem, where

He'd later be crucified, "some Pharisees. . .said to him, 'Get away from here, for Herod wants to kill you'" (Luke 13:31 ESV). Jesus said, "Go and tell that fox, 'Behold, I cast out demons and perform cures today and tomorrow, and the third day I finish my course. *Nevertheless*, I must go on my way today and tomorrow and the day following'" (Luke 13:32-33 ESV, emphasis added).

Both David and Jesus would allow nothing to stand in their way for they knew God was with them, helping them as they walked in His will. It must be something in the blood! But wait! You're a child of God. You too have a nevertheless within you! Use it—in good faith!

Dear Lord, because You are with me, I too have a nevertheless within me. Plant that idea firmly in my mind, Lord, as I walk in Your will and way! Amen.

God is with me, giving me the courage and faith to carry on—nevertheless!

Breakthrough

You have said, Seek My face [inquire for and require My presence as your vital need]. My heart says to You, Your face (Your presence), Lord, will I seek, inquire for, and require [of necessity and on the authority of Your Word]. . . .
"Keep on asking, and you will receive what you ask for. Keep on seeking, and you will find. Keep on knocking, and the door will be opened to you. For everyone who asks, receives. Everyone who seeks, finds. And to everyone who knocks, the door will be opened."
Psalm 27:8 ampc; Luke 11:9-10 nlt

When the Philistines found out David had been made king of Israel, they went looking for him. Unsure of what to do, David sought out advice. He didn't ask his mother, sisters, aunts, uncles, or brothers. He didn't go to the wisest men in his kingdom. He went to God. He "inquired of the Lord" (2 Samuel 5:19 esv), asking if he should go up against them, if God would turn the Philistines over to him. God answered yes to both questions. So David followed God's directions and defeated his enemy. He said, "The Lord has broken through my enemies before me like a breaking flood" (2 Samuel 5:20 esv).

When more Philistines came back to battle against David, he again sought out God for advice. But this time God had a new battle plan. He told David to go circle around to the rear of the enemy. Then to come against them opposite some mulberry trees. "When you hear a sound

like marching feet in the tops of the poplar trees, be on the alert! That will be the signal that the LORD is moving ahead of you to strike down the Philistine army" (2 Samuel 5:24 NLT). David did as God instructed and once more enjoyed victory!

Every time David sought out God's advice—and followed it—he was successful. The same thing will be true of you. So, if you're not sure what to do, go to God. Seek His advice. But never allow your thoughts, ideas, or game plans to drown out God's. Follow His advice—word for word—not your own. When you do, you, like David, will have amazing breakthroughs!

Here I am, Lord, with a load of questions. I'm asking, seeking out Your advice. I'm knocking on the door of Your consultation room. Tell me what to do. Then help me follow Your instructions to the letter. In Jesus' name I pray, amen.

Seeking God's wisdom and plan, I will have a breakthrough!

Seeking Comfort

*As one whom his mother comforts, so I will
comfort you; you shall be comforted. . . .
All praise to the God. . .of all healing counsel! He comes alongside
us when we go through hard times, and before you know it, he brings
us alongside someone else who is going through hard times so that
we can be there for that person just as God was there for us.*

ISAIAH 66:13 ESV; 2 CORINTHIANS 1:3-4 MSG

When someone suffers a loss, a betrayal, or rejection, he or she may
react in various ways. It all depends on the intensity of the trouble, the
various aspects of the situation. Perhaps a person may not even seek
comfort from others, thinking, *No one can possibly understand what I'm
going through.* Oddly enough, that thought does hold a ring of truth.
For each person's situation *is* different. Each person has her own unique
circumstances, cast of characters, and personal history. Yet God assures
you that He will and can comfort you—no matter what your situation.
And He does this so that you can then come alongside someone else
who's going through some hard times.

Yet, for comfort, people often look to God last. Esau, betrayed by
his brother Jacob, comforted himself with the intention of killing him
(Genesis 27:42). The evil King Ahab needed solace because a man wouldn't
sell him his vineyard. So Queen Jezebel comforted her husband by
having the vineyard owner killed, allowing Ahab to have what he wanted

(1 Kings 21). In Psalm 77:2, the psalmist's soul refused to be comforted. His heart was so downcast that no thoughts that came into his mind gave him any relief. Not even Jeremiah could comfort himself (Jeremiah 8:18). Job's friends offered him consolation but apparently did a lousy job, for he calls them "wearisome and miserable comforters" (Job 16:2 AMPC).

When you need comfort, go to God *first*, before you look to friends, family, food, revenge, or possessions for solace. Pour out your heart to Him. Talk to Jesus who, Himself betrayed, rejected, and murdered, knows *exactly* what you're going through. Commune with the Holy Spirit, a.k.a., the Comforter. Then praise God for coming alongside you, helping you catch your breath, calm down, and be healed. Sometime later, when you're ready, watch and wait for the opportunity God will give you to comfort someone else, just as God has comforted you.

I praise You, Lord, for giving me Your comfort in times of trouble.
Now make me ready, willing, and able to give
someone else the care they need!

During hard times, God will give me comfort.

Power Walk

Even though the fig trees have no blossoms, and there are no grapes on the vines; even though the olive crop fails, and the fields lie empty and barren; even though the flocks die in the fields, and the cattle barns are empty, yet I will rejoice in the LORD! . . .
I pray that God, the source of hope, will fill you completely with joy and peace because you trust in him. Then you will overflow with confident hope through the power of the Holy Spirit.

HABAKKUK 3:17-18; ROMANS 15:13 NLT

If only I could rule the world, everything would be just dandy. Ever had that thought?

Habakkuk did. In his short three-chapter book, this prophet wanted to tell God how to run His world. Habakkuk rails about injustices. He complains about how things are going. He wonders why God is so silent.

God responds by telling Habakkuk that He's working on things. The prophet just needs to be patient.

Habakkuk finally asks God to once more reveal His power to this world. Most importantly, he tells God he trusts Him. That even though some hard times look like they're just around the corner, even though trees won't bloom, the vines bear no fruit, crops fail, and herd and flocks are gone, still Habakkuk will trust and hope in God and His plan. He will have joy.

If circumstances have left you with thoughts of hopelessness

and sorrow, making you feel helpless and hapless, take this prayer of Habakkuk's to heart—and mind! Remember the power of God. How He has plans for you to give you hope (Jeremiah 29:11) and is working to bring good to you (Romans 8:28). Remind yourself who God is: "The Lord God is my Strength, my personal bravery, *and* my invincible army; He makes my feet like hinds' feet and will make me to walk [not to stand still in terror, but to walk] *and* make [spiritual] progress upon my high places" (Habakkuk 3:19 AMPC)!

Trust. In God. In God you must trust. No matter what you may think the future holds, no matter what your circumstances were yesterday or are today, trust that God's plan is the best plan. And all is going to be more than well!

Lord, no matter what is happening in this life, I rejoice in You!
I trust You! For You are my strength, my invincible force.
You give me the power to walk in confidence! I revel in
the peace, hope, and joy You provide. Amen.

God is my source of power and hope.

Forever Guide in Life

This is God, our God forever and ever. He will guide us forever. . . .
"It's urgent that you listen carefully to this: Anyone here who believes
what I am saying right now and aligns himself with the Father, who has
in fact put me in charge, has at this very moment the real, lasting life
and is no longer condemned to be an outsider. This person has taken a
giant step from the world of the dead to the world of the living."
PSALM 48:14 ESV; JOHN 5:24 MSG

The older you get, the more you start thinking about death. Not just any death, but your own. Amid this process, a few anxious or fearful thoughts may begin to take root as you wonder when it might be, how it might be. Yet you need not worry about death. Why? Because you're a believer in God, Jesus, and the Spirit. And because you're a believer, you're already, right now in this moment, on your eternal journey! It began the moment you invited Jesus into your life.

Of course, there will come a time when your spirit leaves its vessel, your body, and rises up into the heavenlies. But there's no reason to fear that either. For the Bible gives you glimpses of what you'll see when (or even before) you get there.

Stephen was a man "full of faith and of the Holy Spirit" (Acts 6:5 ESV) and had such an effective ministry that he was charged with blasphemy and brought before the Sandhedrin council. There Stephen delivered a long speech, at the end of which he called his listeners "stiff-necked

people, uncircumcised in heart and ears" who "always resist the Holy Spirit" (Acts 7:51 ESV).

Council members, not liking what they'd heard, were enraged. But Stephen "full of the Holy Spirit, gazed into heaven and saw the glory of God, and Jesus standing at the right hand of God" (Acts 7:55 ESV).

You too have the Spirit dwelling within you. And Jesus says you have already "taken a giant step from the world of the dead to the world of the living." And when you and your spirit make the final transition from your body and into heaven, the Spirit will still be with you. Jesus will greet you. And your God, your forever-Guide, will welcome you with open arms.

Because of You, Lord, I need not fear death for I am already on my forever journey to You. In Jesus' name I pray, amen.

In God, I'm living my forever life.

Back on Track

Thus says the Lord: Do not be afraid because
of the words which you have heard....
Trust and take refuge in Him....
The Temple was filled with smoke from God's glory and power.
Isaiah 37:6 ampc; Psalm 64:10 ampc; Revelation 15:8 nlt

In a previous reading, the miracle-working prophet Elijah became full of despair and discouragement (see pages 36-37). This happened shortly after a mountaintop experience where he'd challenged the prophets of Baal. Praying down God's might, Elijah proved the false god Baal's deafness and powerlessness. Then he killed hundreds of Baal's prophets.

Soon after that, Queen Jezebel, a Baal worshiper, threatened to kill Elijah, saying, "May the gods strike me and even kill me if by this time tomorrow I have not killed you just as you killed them" (1 Kings 19:2 nlt). Fearing for his life, Elijah ran into the wilderness, sat down, and told God, "That's it. I'm done. Kill me now. I'm no better than my ancestors," then fell asleep. An angel of God fed him, giving Elijah the strength to travel to another mountain.

There, in the quiet stillness, God came to Elijah, asking, "What are you doing here?" Elijah related how much he'd done for God. That His people had abandoned Him. That he was the only one left, faithful to God, and now someone was out to kill him. God told Elijah to go back the way he came. To get back on *His* track by anointing two kings and

then anointing Elisha to be his assistant and eventual replacement.

Finally, God said something very interesting: "I will preserve 7,000 others in Israel who have never bowed down to Baal or kissed him!" (1 Kings 19:18 NLT). *God is telling Elijah that his thinking he was the only faithful prophet left was a lie!*

After his mountaintop experience, Elijah, amazed at God's power, must have been exhilarated yet exhausted. But then he allowed Queen Jezebel's death threat to get stuck in his head. In the process, his fear overrode his faith and then depression took him down. Only after God is sure Elijah is going to hear Him does He open his ears to the truth.

When fear overrides your faith, go to God. Trust that He'll tend to you, strengthen you, and lead your thoughts back to His truth and way.

Examine my thoughts, Lord. Rid me of all untruths so that I can gain Your perspective, find peace, and continue in Your strength. Amen.

God's truth gets me back on track!

Loved Back

You have loved back my life from the pit of corruption
and nothingness, for You have cast all my sins behind Your back. . . .
God showed his great love for us by sending Christ to die for us
while we were still sinners. . . . Overwhelming victory is ours
through Christ, who loved us. And I am convinced that
nothing can ever separate us from God's love.
ISAIAH 38:17 AMPC; ROMANS 5:8; 8:37-38 NLT

However great your troubles, sickness, worries, actions, words, and loneliness—whatever experience and thoughts bring you to the end of yourself—God will love back your life, time and time again.

In the days of Judges, "There was no king in Israel. . . . Each man did what he thought was right" (Judges 17:6 NLV). And each time the people did what they thought was right—instead of what God had *told* them was right—they ended up in trouble. Big trouble. But then they would cry out to God. And He would rescue them. He would love back their lives from the pit of destruction.

God sent Jonah to tell the people of Nineveh that they and their city would be destroyed. But then they and their king fasted, mourned their coming demise, and began turning from their evil ways. "God saw their works. . .and God revoked His [sentence of] evil. . .[for He was comforted and eased concerning them]" (Jonah 3:10 AMPC).

When Jesus saw a widow mourning her only son, "He had compassion

on her and said to her, Do not weep" (Luke 7:13 AMPC). He told the young man to rise from his coffin. And he did. Jesus then gave him back to his mother.

Jesus had compassion on the hungry (Matthew 15:32), the discouraged (Matthew 9:36), and the blind (Matthew 20:34). And He expressed extreme compassion and love at the passing of Lazarus. Hearing of his death and seeing his sisters mourning him, "Jesus wept" (John 11:35 ESV). He then loved back his life, raising Lazarus from the dead, and demonstrating the glory of God.

Today, meditate on how much God loves you. Consider how often He loves your life back from the darkness. Then rise up and walk in His light.

Dispel my negative thoughts, my doubts, my fears, and my missteps. Lovingly bring me back to doing what is right in Your eyes and mind. Amen.

God loves my life back from darkness.

God Stands By

*When you pass through the waters, I will be with you; and through
the rivers, they shall not overwhelm you; when you walk through fire
you shall not be burned, and the flame shall not consume you. . . .
No one came to stand by me, but all deserted me.
May it not be charged against them! But the
Lord stood by me and strengthened me.*
ISAIAH 43:2; 2 TIMOTHY 4:16-17 ESV

Just when you think you're all alone, when you believe that no one is
ready, willing, or able to stand by your side, when you are sure you've
been totally abandoned, think again!

Today, in this very moment, get it clear in your mind that no matter
what you are going through, God is standing right beside you. His very
presence, power, light, love, and wisdom are pumping strength into
you, enabling you to do what He's called you to do. And right now that
might be a call for you to rest. Or to rise up. To take that next step. To
be encouraged knowing that you, His daughter, are not and never will
be alone.

As you go through deep waters, God is fighting the undertow with you.
He will not allow you to be swept under by the current or toppled over
by the next wave. As you face rivers of difficulty, God will not allow you to
drown. When you walk through the fires of oppression, discrimination, and
ill-treatment, He will make sure you're neither scorched nor consumed

When you first look around at the people who have left you, you may panic. But when you then look at your situation from God's perspective, you'll realize you've got the most powerful force of love and might standing right next to you, giving you all the strength you need. At the same time, God will pour into you all the love you need to forgive those who have deserted you.

God will always be with you. Because you are precious in His eyes (Isaiah 43:4). So be brave. Fear nothing. Understand the fact that God has called you by your very name. You are not just some lone, weak, helpless woman but His possession. You are the daughter He loves to the moon and back! Live like it!

Thank You, Lord, for standing by me. For always being with me, through thick and thin. In You, I find the strength, power, and love I want, need, and cherish. Amen.

God stands by me and strengthens me.

Seek, Do, Wait, Receive!

The Lord is good to those who wait hopefully and expectantly for Him,
to those who seek Him [inquire of and for Him and require Him by
right of necessity and on the authority of God's word]. It is good
that one should hope in and wait quietly for the
salvation (the safety and ease) of the Lord. . . .
So do not throw away this confident trust in the Lord.
Remember the great reward it brings you!
LAMENTATIONS 3:25-26 AMPC; HEBREWS 10:35 NLT

Do you face life with confidence in God or lose faith at the first sign of trouble? Do you trust God to be good to you or believe He'll bestow on you the bare minimum? Do you expect God to come through or have you already given up?

It's easy to allow dark thoughts to break down your confidence, trust, and hope in God as you wait on Him. Yet His Word makes it clear "You must be willing to wait without giving up. After you have done what God wants you to do, God will give you what He promised you" (Hebrews 10:36 NLV).

Norman Vincent Peale implored people to "have a sincere desire to serve God and mankind, and stop doubting, stop thinking negatively. Simply start living by faith, pray earnestly and humbly, and get into the habit of looking expectantly for the best." And that's just what the prophet Elijah did!

God had told Elijah to tell King Ahab He would soon send rain! So Elijah did, going so far as to tell Ahab, "I hear a mighty rainstorm coming!" (1 Kings 18:41 NLT). After climbing Mount Carmel, Elijah bowed down and prayed. Seven times he told his servant to "go and look out toward the sea" (1 Kings 18:43 NLT). Six times the servant came back to say he'd seen nothing. But the seventh time, the servant said, "I saw a little cloud about the size of a man's hand rising from the sea" (1 Kings 18:44 NLT). Shortly after that, "the sky was black with clouds. A heavy wind brought a terrific rainstorm" (1 Kings 18:45 NLT).

As you wait on God, do so quietly, confidently expecting Him to work in your life. But don't sit on your hands, expecting Him to do it all. Seek out what God wants you to do, do it, and then receive your reward!

Lord, I'm doing what You ask, then waiting on You,
knowing You will come through! Amen.

In God I seek, expecting great rewards!

Called, Chosen, and Blessed

Silence is praise to you, Zion-dwelling God, and also obedience.
You hear the prayer in it all. . . . Blessed are the chosen! Blessed the
guest at home in your place! We expect our fill of good
things in your house, your heavenly manse. . . .
The Lamb will conquer. . .for he is Lord of lords and King of kings,
and those with him are called and chosen and faithful."

PSALM 65:1, 4 MSG; REVELATION 17:14 ESV

Kids are thrilled, surging with joy, when they're picked for a team. When someone calls their name, chooses them above all others, kids never wonder if they'll be picked the next time around. They only live for this moment, hoping and praying to meet their captain's expectations.

You too have been chosen. By God. To play on His team. Ages ago. Before the earth was even formed (Ephesians 1:4). And when you were first chosen, you experienced that initial thrill of a new love. But since that time, you may have become distracted from your Chooser. You're so busy serving God that you've wandered away—in thought, word, and deed—from the intimacy you once shared with Jesus (Revelation 2:4).

Perhaps its time to realign your thoughts and life. To get close to Jesus once more, resettling your focus on Him, making Him your first priority.

Today, instead of just going through the motions of prayer and praise, dig down deep. Sit in silence before Jesus. Imagine laying your head on His shoulder. Bask in His love and presence. Snuggle up close. If your

thoughts begin to go astray, refocus your mind by calling up a Bible verse that will help you turn back to Him. Feel His left hand under your head and His right hand embracing you (Song of Solomon 2:6 AMPC). Sing to Him your desire and praise (Song of Solomon 2:15 AMPC). Rekindle that relationship with your beloved Lord.

Thank You for blessing me, Lord, making me a guest in Your house. As one of Your faithful followers, called, chosen, and blessed, I know I can expect good things to come from Your hand, that You, my Captain, will conquer all. Yet now, in this moment, all I want to do is be with You, loving You. So I'm going deep, snuggling up next to You. Ah. What a blessing, what a Love! Amen.

Called, chosen, and blessed by God, my joy lies in loving Jesus above all else!

All Things

*He will feed His flock like a shepherd: He will gather
the lambs in His arm, He will carry them in His bosom
and will gently lead those that have their young. . . .
May the God of peace—who brought up from the dead our
Lord Jesus, the great Shepherd of the sheep. . .—may
he equip you with all you need for doing his will.*
ISAIAH 40:11 AMPC; HEBREWS 13:20-21 NLT

When you're tired, stressed, or sick, your thoughts may become not so
much negative as muddled. Jumbled to the point where you're not sure
who or what you want, much less where to go. Fortunately, your God
knows not only your thoughts but exactly who and what you need, and
when and where you'll need it. And will provide for you accordingly.

Isaiah 40:10 talks about God's might and power akin to a king. It
then describes God as a benefactor who rewards and compensates His
people. Verse 11 likens God to a shepherd who will gather you in His
arms, carry you, or gently lead you. The Bible makes it clear your God
will supply you with whatever aspect of Him you need—Provider, King,
Spirit, Protector, Anchor, Shepherd, Fortress, Light, Love, etc.

God will also lead you down only the pathway He knows you can
handle. Exodus 13:17 (NLV) says, "When Pharaoh had let the people go,
God did not lead them by the way of the land of the Philistines, even
when that was nearer. For God said, 'The people may change their

minds when they see war, and return to Egypt.'" God then appeared to His people in the form of pillars—a cloud by day and fire by night so the Israelites wouldn't lose their way (Exodus 13:21).

Just as the apostle Paul became all things to all people, so that he might save some (1 Corinthians 9:22), God becomes all things to you so that He can save you, no matter where or when.

So when your thoughts seem muddled, when you're full of uncertainty, go to God. Ask Him to direct you to His Word, to show you who or what aspect of Him you need—Shepherd, King, Benefactor, etc. Then pray, trusting He will appear and lead you down the safest path.

Lord, my Shepherd, God, and King, be with me in all Your many aspects. Show me the way I should go as You walk before, beside, and behind. Amen.

God is exactly Who I need, when and where I need Him.

Gripes vs. Gratitude

*The foreign rabble who were traveling with the Israelites began
to crave the good things of Egypt. And the people
of Israel also began to complain. . . .
Do everything readily and cheerfully—no bickering, no second-guessing
allowed! Go out into the world uncorrupted, a breath of fresh air
in this squalid and polluted society. Provide people with
a glimpse of good living and of the living God.*
NUMBERS 11:4 NLT; PHILIPPIANS 2:14-15 MSG

Complainers. They can be tiresome and frustrating. No one wants to be around them.

When the Israelites complained to Moses about not having enough to eat, he complained about them to God. He begged for God's mercy, wondering what he'd done "to deserve the burden of all these people" (Numbers 11:11 NLT). He claimed this load of people was too heavy for him, telling God, "If this is how you intend to treat me, just go ahead and kill me. Do me a favor and spare me this misery!" (Numbers 11:15 NLT). Thankfully, God dealt with the situation. He provided helpers for Moses. God also provided food for the people. When they became greedy gatherers, their punishment, in the form of a plague, soon followed. But we digress. . . .

The point is that, just as much as we hate to hear people complain, we too can be complainers, in our speech *and* thoughts. If we were honest

we'd realize that sometimes we sound just like the Israelites. Especially when *we* don't get what we want, or feel *we've* been treated badly. When *we're* dissatisfied on some level and are ready to blame someone else for *our* misfortune or lack. Our complaints reveal it's all about us!

Today, keep an extra vigilant watch on your speech and thoughts. Ask God to highlight any complaints. When one arises, take it before God in the form of a prayer. Let Him know where and why you're unhappy. Ask Him to give you a new perspective on the situation. Consider how much you have to be thankful for. As you do so, your focus will shift from you to others. Your gripes will abate and second-guessing stop. Cheerfulness and gratefulness will become the rule of your day. To the benefit of yourself and everyone around you.

Lord, I never realized how much internal (and sometimes external) whining I do! Remind me to come to You with any complaints I have. Give me a new perspective. Exchange my griping for gratitude for my many blessings. Amen.

God changes my gripes to gratitude!

The Ultimate Job

Whatever your hand finds to do, do it with all your strength. . . .
Do your best. Work from the heart for your real Master, for God,
confident that you'll get paid in full when you come into
your inheritance. Keep in mind always that the
ultimate Master you're serving is Christ.
ECCLESIASTES 9:10 NLV; COLOSSIANS 3:23 MSG

In the second book of Kings, we read about Naaman, a commander of the Syrian army. Although a mighty man of valor, he was also a leper. Living with him was a little girl from Israel, who'd been captured during a Syrian raid. She worked as a servant to Naaman's wife. Although basically a prisoner there, the little Jewish girl cared about her master and his health. So she told her mistress, "Oh, if only my master could meet the prophet of Samaria, he would be healed of his skin disease" (2 Kings 5:3 MSG). Apparently Naaman's nameless wife told her husband what her nameless servant girl had said. In turn, "Naaman told the king" (2 Kings 5:4 NLT) and received permission to visit Elisha.

The story continues with Naaman finding Elisha and, after a false start during which the commander had to swallow his pride, following Elisha's instructions. In doing so, Naaman is not only healed physically—"his skin became as healthy as the skin of a young child" (2 Kings 5:14 NLT)—but spiritually as he becomes a humble and childlike believer in God.

All this is due to the attitude of a little girl with a big faith, physically

a prisoner but spiritually a free spirit in God. She, a nameless slave, never demonstrates a bad attitude or negative thoughts. She never bemoans her status or tasks. Instead, she readily does what she can to follow God, working for Him with all her heart, doing her best to serve Him and others in love.

Today, as you work, consider this selfless and godly servant girl. Ask God to transform your thoughts, to help you do your best, to work from the heart, keeping in mind that you're true Master is Christ as you live out His Word, spreading His love and light.

Lord, my thoughts and attitude toward work aren't always positive.
Help me keep in mind that You are my true Master, Jesus!
And my ultimate job is to do my best, to work with all
my heart, for You. In Your name I pray, amen.

Working for God, I find and do my best!

Fearless and Focused

Fear not [there is nothing to fear], for I am with you; do not look around you in terror and be dismayed, for I am your God. I will strengthen and harden you to difficulties, yes, I will help you; yes, I will hold you up and retain you with My [victorious] right hand of rightness and justice. . . .
The Lord said to Paul one night in a vision, "Do not be afraid, but go on speaking and do not be silent, for I am with you, and no one will attack you to harm you, for I have many in this city who are my people."

ISAIAH 41:10 AMPC; ACTS 18:9-10 ESV

Fear-filled thoughts can lead to different levels of panic. There's the short flash of panic you get when you realize you'll be late for an appointment. Then there's panic of a longer duration when you learn your child (with her own kids in tow) may move in with you. Then there's the full-blown panic when you hear the train coming and your car has stalled on the tracks.

We're not sure what level of panic the apostle Paul attained. We can assume it was relatively high. Why else would God come to him in a vision? But there's one thing we do know: Paul took God at His word and his ministry in Corinth flourished. Have you taken God at His word?

In Isaiah 41:10, there are only two things God tells you to do: (1) don't fear and (2) don't look around and freak out. Why shouldn't you fear? Because "there is nothing to fear." Why is there nothing to fear? Because God is with you. Why should you not "look around you in terror and be dismayed"? Because God wants you to keep your focus on Him.

While you're staying fearless and focused on God, He promises to
• **be with you** • **be your God** • **strengthen and harden you** • **help you** •
and hold you up with His right hand. You do your part, let God do His,
and everything will turn out right. For as you follow God's direction, His
presence will lead you to His peace.

---

*I'm tired, Lord, of letting my thoughts run away with me, leading me
into fear, then panic. So I'm turning to You. With eyes, mind,
and heart on You, I know all will be well. In Jesus' name, amen.*

I have nothing to fear for God is with me.

Prompted by Faith

It was by faith that Moses' parents hid him for three months when
he was born. They saw that God had given them an unusual child,
and they were not afraid to disobey the king's command. . . .
When she could no longer hide him, she got a basket made of papyrus
reeds and waterproofed it with tar and pitch. She put the baby in the
basket and laid it among the reeds along the bank of the Nile River.
HEBREWS 11:23; EXODUS 2:3 NLT

Pharaoh, the king of Egypt, had just issued an edict, commanding that all male Hebrew newborns were to be cast into the Nile at birth. But every daughter could live. Not the best time to be a pregnant Hebrew woman.

Yet there stood Jochebed, the mother of Aaron and Miriam, carrying another child. But she allowed no fearful thoughts to override her faith. Instead, she and her husband disobeyed the king's command. Because of their immense and unshakable faith, amid the height of the Pharaoh's cruelty to God's people, Moses their deliverer was born.

Jochebed hid her little one for three months. Then she took another leap of faith. She made a waterproof basket, put Moses inside, and set him—a helpless baby—afloat on the Nile River, turning her son over to the care of God.

Meanwhile, Miriam watched from a distance, to see what would happen to her baby brother. From her hiding place, she saw the Pharaoh's daughter come down to the river to wash. When the princess saw the

basket, she had a maid fetch it. Seeing the beautiful, now crying baby within his ark, the princess took pity on him.

Miriam bravely came forward, asking if she could find a Hebrew woman to nurse the infant. Pharaoh's daughter told her to do so and soon Jochebed found herself hired to nurse her own child.

It was faith that prompted Moses' parents to conceal the child who would someday save God's people. It was faith and hope that prompted Jochebed to prepare a water-tight basket for her child, place it in the Nile, and send her daughter to watch over it.

When you allow faith and hope to prompt you, rather than fear-filled thoughts, God can and will do mighty things by and through you—even turn an enemy into a lifesaver.

Help me, Lord, to not focus on fears but my faith, thus opening the door to You working miracles in and through me. In Jesus' name, amen.

My faith opens the door to God's miracles.

Heart Guard

Keep and guard your heart with all vigilance and above
all that you guard, for out of it flow the springs of life. . . .
"What you say flows from what is in your heart."
PROVERBS 4:23 AMPC; LUKE 6:45 NLT

Miriam was a devoted daughter and sister as she stood on the banks of the Nile. She watched and waited until her baby brother Moses was taken off the water by Pharaoh's daughter. Miriam then bravely asked the princess if she could find a Hebrew nurse for the babe, bringing back her mother who was hired on the spot.

Later, after brother Moses led the Israelites out of Egypt, Miriam, now a prophetess, led the women in a celebration song (Exodus 15). But then something went sour in Miriam's mind and heart.

Unhappy with their brother's choice of wife, Miriam and Aaron spoke out against Moses. They said, out of apparent bitterness and jealousy, "Is it only through Moses that GOD speaks? Doesn't he also speak through us?" (Numbers 12:2 MSG). And God heard what they said. Uh-oh.

At the Tent of Meeting, God explained to the siblings—Aaron, Miriam, and Moses—that, unlike other prophets, to whom He speaks through dreams and visions, He speaks directly to Moses. Then, still angered with Aaron and Miriam, God departed. When His cloud rose above the tent, Miriam was "leprous, as white as snow" (Numbers 12:10 AMPC).

Aaron pleaded to Moses to help her. Moses, in his love for his sister,

prayed, begging God for her healing. God did promptly heal her. But after comparing Miriam's words against Moses to the actions of a daughter spitting in her father's face, God ordered her to be sent outside the camp for seven days as punishment. The people waited for her return, then decamped.

By praying for her healing, Moses chose to return Miriam's evil with good. That demonstration of his love and forgiveness must have touched Miriam's heart. "Doubtless the leprosy of Miriam's mind departed with the leprosy of her body" (Edith Deen, *All the Women of the Bible*, p. 61).

Keep an eye on what's in your heart. Make sure no grumblings, thoughts of jealousy, bitterness, or discontentment are festering within. For if they remain unchecked, chances are they'll flow out in a way that will *not* please God.

God, keep me free of thoughts that may become dangerous seedlings within my heart, which will only lead to wrong words without. Amen.

Today I'm planting good seeds of thought in my mind.

Carried Day by Day

Blessed be the Lord, Who bears our burdens and carries
us day by day, even the God Who is our salvation!
Selah [pause, and calmly think of that]! . . .
Therefore humble yourselves [demote, lower yourselves in your own
estimation] under the mighty hand of God, that in due time He may
exalt you, casting the whole of your care [all your anxieties, all your
worries, all your concerns, once and for all] on Him, for He cares
for you affectionately and cares about you watchfully.
PSALM 68:19; 1 PETER 5:6-7 AMPC

Have you ever had a day where all you wanted to do was crawl into your mom or dad's arms, have them lift you up, hold you, carry you until. . .well, until you regained your calm, rest, strength, joy, contentment, whatever it was you needed? Perhaps it wasn't a parent but a grandparent, a big brother or sister, a foster parent, an aunt, or an uncle who you could run to. But perhaps that person is unable to play that role anymore. Or perhaps you think you're too old to go running to someone. Maybe you're the stiff-upper-lip type, not wanting to show any sign of weakness.

When you think you can handle all the problems, carry all the burdens, and don't need anyone to help you take another step, stop and *really* think. Are those thoughts true? Because God's Word says you *can't* handle all the problems and carry all the burdens. He didn't design you

that way. You've been made to be dependent upon God—for everything! Including nurturing.

Yet the best part of all this is that no matter who you are or who is or isn't in your life right now, there's one person who will always be there for you. God. When all you want to do (or all you can do) is cry, go to God. When you have no more strength, go to God. When you can't go one more step because your mind is in such a muddle, go to God. Turn everything, including yourself, over to Him. For once you totally surrender yourself to God, you'll be totally uplifted.

Today, God is bending down to you, examining your face. Look up and surrender to His presence. Reach out for His loving embrace. Crawl into His arms, allowing Him to lift, hold, soothe, and carry you. Pause, and calmly think of that!

I'm reaching out for You, Lord. Lift me. Hold me. Carry me. Amen.

God carries me.

Mountain Movers

Fear not. . . . I will help you, says the Lord. . . . I will make you to be a new, sharp, threshing instrument which has teeth; you shall thresh the mountains and beat them small, and shall make the hills like chaff. You shall winnow them, and the wind shall carry them away. . . . Whoever says to this mountain, Be lifted up and thrown into the sea! and does not doubt at all in his heart but believes that what he says will take place, it will be done for him.
ISAIAH 41:14-16; MARK 11:23 AMPC

God is in the business of transforming you, molding you into the woman He designed you to be. But before He can make any alterations, you must surrender to Him. Fix your attention on Him, allowing Him to renew you—body, soul, and mind. Only then can you be changed, remade!

Through Isaiah, God voices His desire to make you an obstacle overcomer, an amazingly powerful force that can remove whatever mountains lie between you and His purpose for you.

To that end, God is going to strengthen you, to make you be a thresher with sharp teeth. So sharp that you can chew up the mountains and hills impeding your path. You'll crush them like dry cut grass that the wind will blow away!

Thousands of years later, Jesus explains obstacle-overcoming capabilities in a different way. Instead of chewing up a mountain, you're removing it, by telling it to be lifted up and fall into the sea. Jesus promises

that if you believe and have confidence in God, if you hold no doubts in your heart—and mind—what you say *will* happen. Because God, the master of making the impossible possible, will *make* it happen.

If you want to have any chance of being an obstacle overcomer, you cannot read today's verses and think to yourself, *Yeah, right. That may work for some women but not for me.* For by entertaining such thoughts, you're *planting* an obstacle (in this case, doubt) between you and the God who empowers you. Woman, this cannot be!

Instead, present yourself to God. Allow Him to mold you, knowing there's nothing to be afraid of. For He will not give you anything you will not be able to handle. God is here to help you. To transform you. To empower you. Ready? Let's move some mountains!

I come before You, Lord, bowing before You. Remove any doubts from me so that I can be Your obstacle overcomer. Amen.

Through God's power, I overcome obstacles!

The Quencher

*Come, buy [priceless, spiritual] wine and milk without money and
without price [simply for the self-surrender that accepts the blessing]
. . . . Incline your ear [submit and consent to the divine will] and come to
Me; hear, and your soul will revive. . . . Seek, inquire for, and require the
Lord while He may be found [claiming Him by necessity
and by right]; call upon Him while He is near. . . .
Come! And let everyone come who is thirsty [who is painfully conscious
of his need of those things by which the soul is refreshed, supported,
and strengthened]; and whoever [earnestly] desires to do it, let him
come, take, appropriate, and drink the water of Life without cost.*

ISAIAH 55:1, 3, 6; REVELATION 22:17 AMPC

When thoughts are taking you down, seek God. When you feel as if you're stuck mentally, emotionally, or spiritually, seek Jesus. When you need to be lifted up out of yourself so that you can catch your breath, seek the Spirit.

Access to all three members of the Trinity costs you nothing. All you have to do is surrender yourself. To let God take you over.

Let's face it. This life is unlivable, untenable without God. That's why you picked up this book. You look for direction, you read your Bible, go to church, and pray because you're painfully conscious of your need for things that refresh, support, and strengthen your soul! But that need will not be satisfied if you don't give up your own ego and submit your entire

self—mind, body, soul, and spirit—to God. You will remain unfulfilled if you do not turn away from this world, "but let God transform you into a new person by changing the way you think. Then you will learn to know God's will for you" (Romans 12:2 NLT).

Today, make it a point to quench your spiritual thirst. Submit to God. Surrender yourself to Him. Go to Jesus. Trust, believe, and rely on Him. Seek the Spirit. As you do, you'll find your thoughts bearing fruit, your soul being refreshed. You'll find the support you need to answer God's call and the strength to do His will. And you'll find rivers of living water flowing from your heart.

God, Jesus, and Spirit, I come to You, surrendering myself to You.
Refresh, support, and strengthen my soul. Renew my mind,
so that I can be and do all You desire. In Jesus' name, amen.

As I surrender to God, my soul strengthens.

Isaiah Instructions

*"**Do not fear**, for I am with you. **Do not be afraid, for I am your God.**
I will give you strength, and for sure **I will help you**. Yes, **I will hold you
up with My right hand** that is right and good. . . . **I am the Lord your
God Who holds your right hand**, and Who says to you, '**Do not be
afraid. I will help you.**' **Do not fear**. . . . **I will help you**,"* says the Lord. . . .
*She came and got down before Jesus and worshiped
Him. She said, "Lord, help me!"*

ISAIAH 41:10, 13-14 (EMPHASES ADDED); MATTHEW 15:25 NLV

In Isaiah 41:10, 13-14, God is telling you what He wants you to understand
and then plant in your brainbox.

Four times, God stresses you're not to be afraid. Three times,
He promises to help you. Twice He identifies Himself as your God. And
one time each He tells you He'll hold you up with *His* right hand and
will take you by *your* right hand. All this to assure you that you need not
fear or believe yourself helpless—now or ever.

To help build up that assurance deep within, rid yourself of fear-filled
thoughts. Envision God going before you, scouting out the road ahead.
Feeling your presence, He turns around and stops to look behind and
beside you. He then bends down, puts His lips to your ear, and whispers,
"Do not fear. Do not be frightened by anything or anyone. I've got this.
I've got you. Do not fear."

As He turns back to check the way ahead, say to yourself, "I am not

afraid. God has me safe in His hand." Repeat these two sentences at least three times a day—morning, noon, and night.

To rid yourself of any thoughts of helplessness, place yourself in Jesus' presence. Bow before Him, worshipping Him. Then say, "Lord, help me!" Envision Jesus reaching out His right arm to pull you up into His secure embrace. He smiles as He lifts your feet up off the ground and says, "No worries, sister in Christ! I've got a good grip on you. I'm here to help you do whatever you need to do!" As He trudges off with you securely in His hold, repeat to yourself, "Jesus has me in His hands. He's constantly helping me!"

Lord, knowing You're with me, I need not fear or feel helpless! Amen!

In God, I have constant courage and help!

Transformed by the Shepherd

The Lord is my Shepherd [to feed, guide, and shield me], I shall
not lack. He makes me lie down in [fresh, tender] green
pastures; He leads me beside the still and restful waters.
He refreshes and restores my life (my self)....
I am the Good Shepherd; and I know and recognize
My own, and My own know and recognize Me....
Your Shepherd, the Guardian of your souls.

PSALM 23:1-3 AMPC; JOHN 10:14 AMPC; 1 PETER 2:25 NLT

Psalm 23—written by David, the shepherd-boy king—is the best known of all psalms. Perhaps that's because its words exude truth and comfort.

The psalm begins, "The Lord is my shepherd." Not *was* or *will be* but *is* your shepherd, every moment. And this Lord Shepherd doesn't just half-heartedly guide you or carelessly walk with you; He's focused and vigilant. He nourishes you, gives you direction, and protects you. With Him taking the lead, you will not lack any good thing. For He continually provides you with everything you need—including rest!

Your Good Shepherd insists you lie down in a very lush and comfortable place. He takes you to water that is still, silent, peaceful. (Keep in mind that sheep, like humans, are a bit skittish. Rushing water frightens them. So for them to drink, the water must be still.) All so that you can catch your breath and be replenished. It is there, in that blessed place of peace, rest, and safety that God can transform your heart, mind,

and soul. As you commune with Him, the inner you is restored.

Jesus identifies Himself as your Good Shepherd. He knows and recognizes you, just as you know and recognize Him. He wants you to understand, to take it as a fact that He's the Guardian of your soul.

In this moment, allow God to be your Shepherd. Trust that He will feed, guide, and shield you. Accept that you'll never lack any good thing from His hand. Then imagine lying down in His fresh, green meadow, drinking your fill by the still waters. Resting under His watchful care. And you will be transformed.

Be my Good Shepherd, Lord. Feed me, guide me, protect me. Remind me that I will never lack anything. Make me lie down in green pastures. Lead me beside still waters. In You I find my rest, comfort, provision, peace, protection, nourishment, and way. Amen.

God, the Shepherd of my life and Guardian of my soul, is all I need.

God, Rod, and Staff

He leads me in the paths of righteousness [uprightness and right
standing with Him—not for my earning it, but] for His name's sake.
Yes, though I walk through the [deep, sunless] valley of the shadow
of death, I will fear or dread no evil, for You are with me; Your rod
[to protect] and Your staff [to guide], they comfort me. . . .
The Good Shepherd risks and lays down
His [own] life for the sheep.

PSALM 23:3-4; JOHN 10:11 AMPC

Once your Good Shepherd has restored and refreshed your soul, He leads you down a path on which you can do God's work. You rejoice over the duties He's assigned you, the ones He prepared ahead of time that you should do (Ephesians 2:10).

Yet then suddenly, before you know it, you're deep in the valley of darkness. You begin walking a bit slower, unsure of what may be lurking in the shadows. Is it a predator with sharp teeth? Will a tsunami burst between those trees and take out everything in its path? Perhaps a mugger is waiting around the corner. Your heart begins to thump crazily, your mind to race. But then you feel someone squeeze your hand. You look up and see the Shepherd walking beside you. All at once, you fear nothing, dread nothing. He's got His rod to protect you, His staff to guide. You regain your courage. Your shoulders relax, teeth unclench, stomach slackens, and panic abates. Your mind is once more back on

God's wavelength. Your heart beats in time with His. You walk on in His rhythm. Soon your worries and fears are a dim shadow in the distance, nothing that a bit more light won't dissipate.

Because of your Good Shepherd's presence, you're calm once more. For you know He'll do anything, risk everything—including His own life—to save yours. So you've got nothing to worry about.

Woman, this is where you are to be. Walking with God in such a way your minds are aligned and your hearts beat as one.

Today, imagine walking amid a dark valley with the Lord. Allow some of your current fears and worries to crop up. Then imagine your Shepherd beating them off with His rod. Then, with His staff, He leads you to the place of comfort within Him.

---

*Good Shepherd, even when I walk through the dark valleys of life
I know I need not be afraid. For You are with me. Amen.*

Because of God's presence, protection,
and guidance, I fear nothing.

A Well-Set Table

You prepare a table before me in the presence of my enemies. You
anoint my head with oil; my [brimming] cup runs over. Surely or only
goodness, mercy, and unfailing love shall follow me all the days of
my life, and through the length of my days the house of the
Lord [and His presence] shall be my dwelling place. . . .
"Look! Look! God has moved into the neighborhood, making his home
with men and women! They're his people, he's their God. He'll wipe
every tear from their eyes. Death is gone for good—tears gone,
crying gone, pain gone—all the first order of things gone."
PSALM 23:5-6 AMPC; REVELATION 21:3-4 MSG

In these last two verses of Psalm 23, you once more find food and rest, just as you did in verses 1-3. Yet things are a little bit more tense in this situation. For God has prepared a table for you. On it are all the provisions you need—and more!

That's great. God has given you a feast. But it sits in the presence of strife—your enemies, all the things against you.

Yet even there, amid strife, God is blessing you, allowing you to be restored, strengthened, and provided for. He goes even further, anointing your head with the oil of the Holy Spirit! Your cup of God's mercy, love, salvation, grace, and more is running over!

Because God is with you through it all—feeding you, guiding you, shielding you; making you lie down to rest; leading you to the still water

of peace; restoring and refreshing your soul; leading you down the right paths; protecting and guiding you through the dark valleys, giving you the sense of security you need; serving a huge feast amid enemies; reviving you with oil; and overflowing your cup with blessings—you find the hope you need to carry on.

No more can words assail you, thoughts bring you down, ideas lead you down the wrong path. For you are living and walking in your Good Shepherd's presence. You are allowing Him to take the lead, giving Him full reign in your life. That's why you can now say and pray:

You, God, are giving me all the goodness and love I could ever desire, every day of my life! They follow me wherever I go! And will continue to do so as I one day make my home with You. Amen.

God blesses me, even amid strife!

Sleep Like a Rock

I lay down and slept; I wakened again,
for the Lord sustains me. I will not be afraid. . . .
Jesus was sleeping at the back of the boat with his head on a cushion.
The disciples woke him up, shouting, "Teacher, don't you care that we're
going to drown?" When Jesus woke up, he rebuked the wind and said
to the waves, "Silence! Be still!" Suddenly. . .there was a great calm.
PSALM 3:5-6 AMPC; MARK 4:38-39 NLT

At times sleep can be very elusive. You've counted sheep, played games in your head, kept the TV on, but still cannot catch a wink. Worries have overtaken your mind. Fears have wrapped themselves around your soul. What-ifs have weighed down your spirit. It's time to seek wisdom from the Lord. To replace your thoughts, such as, *I'm never going to get a good night's sleep*, with God's truth. To temper your worries, fears, and what-ifs with God's Word to the wise.

Psalm 3 is "A Psalm of David, when he fled from Absalom his son." Absalom, who'd already killed one of his brothers, was trying to overthrow his father's kingship. So he led a rebellion against King David, forcing David to flee his home. In the end, Absalom was killed and David regained his throne. But talk about problems! Would you be able to sleep with all that mayhem going on in your life? Granted, you're not a king. But you could be a queen. . . . If not of a kingdom, perhaps your house.

The point is David *could* sleep. Even amid all this chaos. That's

because he knew God shielded him on all sides, heard his prayer, and sustained him. David says, "I will not be afraid of ten thousands of people who have set themselves against me" (Psalm 3:6 AMPC). David asks God to rise up, ending with "real help comes from GOD. Your blessing clothes your people!" (Psalm 3:8 MSG).

Jesus apparently slept like a rock. Even during a terrific storm, He continued to sleep. Why? Because He had faith in Abba God.

If you have trouble sleeping, tell your worries and head-chatter, "Silence! Be still!" Have faith God is sustaining you, watching over you. Remember times in the past where He's been there for you. Then pray:

"In peace I will both lie down and sleep, for You, Lord, alone make me dwell in safety and confident trust" (Psalm 4:8 AMPC). Amen.

Trusting in God, I sleep in peace.

Opening Up

*"I will pour out my Spirit upon all people. . . . Your old men
will dream dreams, and your young men will see visions." . . .
Joseph, being a just and upright man. . .decided to. . .(divorce) her
quietly and secretly. But as he was thinking this over, behold,
an angel of the Lord appeared to him in a dream, saying. . .
do not be afraid. . . . Then Joseph, being aroused from his
sleep, did as the angel of the Lord had commanded.*

JOEL 2:28 NLT; MATTHEW 1:19-20, 24 AMPC

Joseph must have been shocked when he discovered Mary was pregnant. In those days, adultery was not only embarrassing but grounds for divorce—and punishment (Mosaic Law called for her to be stoned)! So Joseph decided to divorce Mary quietly.

While Joseph was thinking this over, an angel came to him in a dream, telling him not to be afraid but to take Mary as his wife; that she was pregnant by the Holy Spirit; and that she would bear a Son he was to name Jesus.

When Joseph woke, he did just what the angel of the Lord had told him to do, regardless of what the norms of his day demanded. He married Mary, had no relations with her until after her babe was born, and named Him Jesus.

In the middle of this account, Matthew says all these events took place to fulfill God's plan and prophecy (Matthew 1:22-23; Isaiah 7:14).

Yet it's easy to see that Joseph played a key role—*by allowing God to transform him by renewing his mind!*

Initially, Joseph had decided to follow the custom of his day, yet continues to consider possible options when he falls asleep. That opens the door to God making His will known through an angel who lays out God's game plan. Joseph, when he awakens, follows *God's* plan, setting the course for Jesus' safe arrival.

Joseph allowed God to renew his thoughts, transform his mind. And, in the process, he learned "to know God's will. . .which is good and pleasing and perfect" (Romans 12:2 NLT) for him, his family, and the world.

You too are to place your life before God. To not copy the behavior and ways of this world. But to be open to God, to let Him transform you by changing the way you think. Then you'll learn God's good will for you.

My mind is open to You, Lord.
What would you have me do and think? Amen.

Open to God, I'm transformed.

The Prodigal's Transformation

*"I'll give you a new heart, put a new spirit in you. I'll remove
the stone heart from your body and replace it with
a heart that's God-willed, not self-willed." ...
"This son of mine was dead and has now returned
to life. He was lost, but now he is found."*

EZEKIEL 36:26 MSG; LUKE 15:23-24 NLT

In the tale of the Prodigal Son, a landowner's youngest of two sons demands his share of his father's estate. A few days after the father agreed to divide his wealth between the boys, the youngest son leaves home, then, while in a foreign land, goes through all his money. When a famine hits, the son is out of food and friends. Hungry, he gets a job feeding pigs that were eating better than he was!

That's when the prodigal "came to his senses" (Luke 15:17 NLT). Having decided to go home, he rehearses his speech: "Father, I've sinned against God, I've sinned before you; I don't deserve to be called your son. Take me on as a hired hand" (Luke 15:18 MSG). Then he gets up and heads for home.

His father, seeing him coming "while he was still a long way off" (Luke 15:20 ESV), runs to hug and kiss him. The son manages to get out only the first part of his speech before his father interrupts, telling the servants, "Get the best robe, ring, and shoes to put on him. We're going to have a feast to celebrate! Because my son was dead but is now alive,

was lost but is now found!"

During the celebration, the oldest son comes in from the fields. He gripes to his father about how he's always done as told and no feast was ever held for him. The patient and loving father insists everything he has is the elder's. But this is a time to celebrate.

Truly transformed was the youngest son, the one who'd been in trouble but then came to his senses, realizing how much he'd hurt his father and himself by being so self-willed instead of God-willed. Once as good as dead, he now has returned to a true life in God.

No matter how sinful or messed up your past, God has compassion on you. He's watching and waiting for you. Just come to your senses, get up, and run into His arms! Then you too will be transformed—in heart and mind.

I come before You, Lord, humbled. Give me,
your prodigal daughter, a God-willed heart. Amen.

God's compassion renews my heart and mind.

Prayer Posits

Before they call I will answer;
and while they are yet speaking I will hear. . . .
Now faith is the assurance (the confirmation, the title deed)
of the things [we] hope for, being the proof of things [we] do not
see and the conviction of their reality [faith perceiving
as real fact what is not revealed to the senses].

ISAIAH 65:24; HEBREWS 11:1 AMPC

What if you lived your life believing your prayers were already answered?

Do you feel the power of that question? It's transformational!!! Yet isn't that what faith is? Living your life as if God has heard and is answering your request?

It happened to Daniel. While he was still pouring out his heart to God, the angel Gabriel flew in to view and landed right in front of him. He said, "Daniel, I have come to make things plain to you. You had no sooner started your prayer when the answer was given. And now I'm here to deliver the answer to you" (Daniel 9:22–23 MSG).

The childless Hannah, while weeping, prayed for a son. When Eli the priest added his blessing, saying, "Go in peace! May the God of Israel grant the request you have asked of him" (1 Samuel 1:17 NLT), she must have walked away believing because "she went back and began to eat again, and she was no longer sad" (1 Samuel 1:18 NLT). And in due course, her prayer was answered in the birth of her son Samuel.

The servant girl Rhoda and her home-church were praying for Peter's release from jail. Their prayer moved an angel to help him escape. When Peter came knocking on the door of John Mark's mom's house, Rhoda went to answer it. Recognizing Peter's voice, she was so excited to tell everyone he was free that she forgot to open the door, leaving him outside in the street. Her fellow prayers were incredulous, telling her, "You're crazy" (Acts 12:15 MSG). But Peter was indeed free! Their prayers had been answered!

God does answer prayer—even before you begin praying. When you pray, tell yourself God is listening and pays attention to your prayers (Psalm 66:19). Believe Jesus when He says what you ask for—if it pleases Him—will be yours (John 15:7; Mark 11:24; 1 John 5:14-15). Transform your life by believing your prayers have already been answered!

Help increase my faith, Lord. Help me believe that my prayers are being answered—sometimes even before I speak them! Amen!

God answers my prayers before I'm done asking!

Unsettling Transformation

"Everything he does is right, and he does it the right way.
He knows how to turn a proud person into a
humble man or woman." . . .
I ask each one of you not to think more of himself
than he should think. Instead, think in the right way
toward yourself by the faith God has given you.
DANIEL 4:37 MSG; ROMANS 12:3 NLV

Nebuchadnezzar was a pagan Babylonian king. After invading Jerusalem, he brought back some of the nobility of Israel, including Daniel and his friends.

After Daniel, with help from God, interpreted one of Nebuchadnezzar's dreams, the king promoted him. Yet Nebuchadnezzar would not claim allegiance to God.

Later, Nebuchadnezzar required all people to bow down to a golden statue he'd had made. Three of Daniel's friends—Shadrach, Meshach, and Abednego—would only bow to God. So the king had them put into a blazing furnace—out of which God delivered them! Yet still, Nebuchadnezzar wouldn't bow to the Lord of lords.

Then Nebuchadnezzar had another dream, from which Daniel foretold a humiliating situation the king would encounter. A year later, Nebuchadnezzar was walking on the roof of his royal palace, surveying and reviewing all the great things he'd accomplished, attributing his

prosperity to himself. "While the words were still in the king's mouth" (Daniel 4:31 ESV), God said his kingdom would be taken from him, he'd be driven into the wilderness, live with wild animals, eat grass, and more until he learned "that the High God rules human kingdoms and puts whomever he wishes in charge" (Daniel 4:32 MSG). Nebuchadnezzar's nightmare had begun. He ate grass like an ox. His hair grew like an eagle's feathers and his nails like a hawk's claws.

Seven years later, Nebuchadnezzar got back his mind, then blessed and thanked God rather than himself! Once he humbled himself, he regained his kingdom, majesty, and splendor.

Prideful people find it difficult, if not impossible, to present themselves to God as a living offering and allow Him to have full reign over their thoughts. But it's a fact that at some point down the road, God will let them hit rock bottom so they'll realize all they are and have come from His power and hands—not their own!

Today, do a pride check. If needed, ask God to help you be more humble.

Lord, if there is any pride in me, please remove it gently, lovingly.
Help me think more of You and others than myself. Amen.

God lifts the humble.

Rising Above

Fear not; stand still (firm, confident, undismayed) and see the salvation
of the Lord which He will work for you today. For the Egyptians you
have seen today you shall never see again. The Lord will fight for
you, and you shall hold your peace and remain at rest. . . .
Be strong in the Lord [be empowered through your union
with Him]; draw your strength from Him [that strength
which His boundless might provides].
EXODUS 14:13-14; EPHESIANS 6:10 AMPC

God told Moses where to place the Israelites who had just escaped Egypt. The Lord wanted Pharaoh to think they'd be easy pickings. He then stoked up Pharaoh's anger, hardening his heart, which led to the Egyptian king and his chariots bearing down on the Israelites.

Fear impelled God's people to cry out to Moses, asking him why he hadn't just let them die in Egypt! Moses tries to reassure them, saying, "Don't freak out! Stand still, confident. Today you're going to see God's saving power! This enemy coming against you. . .you'll never ever see again. God's going to fight for you. Just stay calm. Hold on to your peace."

God then gave Moses His game plan. "Tell everybody to start walking toward the sea. Then lift up your staff and stretch your hand out to divide the sea. Then My people can walk across on dry ground. Once they're on the other side, I'll bring the water back and drown the enemy! Then those Egyptians will know I'm God!" God's angel then moved behind His

people, acting as a buffer between them and their enemy.

The next morning, the Israelites crossed safely. The sea waters had gone back to normal. And Egyptian bodies lay scattered on the shore. That's when God's people realized His tremendous power. In awe before God, their trust in God and Moses was restored.

When you're fenced in, trapped and troubled on every side, frightened for your life, it's only natural to cry out to God in prayer. To obtain His reassurance. But fear should not move you into a complaint mode, because that implies a disbelief in God's miracles and power.

When you can't get out of your trouble, get into God. When you can't run from your fear, rise above it. Find a place to stand still, neither fighting nor fleeing. Draw your strength from God, and He will not just transform your situation but transform you!

Lord, when thoughts of fear override my faith,
help me stand firm, confident in You. Amen.

My confidence in God brings me power and courage.

Definite Doubts

*"I will lead the blind by a way that they do not know. . .in paths
they do not know. I will turn darkness into light in front of them.
And I will make the bad places smooth. . . . I will not leave them.". . .
The Lord said, "Go over to Straight Street. . . .
Ask for a man. . .named Saul. . . ."
"But Lord," exclaimed Ananias.*
ISAIAH 42:16 NLV; ACTS 9:11, 13 NLT

Saul of Tarsus had been passionately persecuting Christians. But on the road to Damascus, a bright light from heaven came down, felling Saul. It was a close encounter of the Jesus kind. Jesus told him to stop persecuting Him. Then He told the now blind Saul to go into the city and await further instruction.

For three days, Saul didn't eat or drink. Meanwhile, Jesus appeared to His disciple Ananias in a vision. He told him, "Go to Straight Street and ask for Judas's house. There you'll find a man named Saul praying. He's already seen you in a vision, laying your hands on him so he can regain his sight."

Ananias responded with a "But, Lord." This disciple *definitely* had his doubts. After all, he's heard Saul has killed lots of Christians. And now he's got the high priest's authority to arrest more followers of the Way.

It's obvious Ananias's mixture of fear and doubt made him hesitate to do what Jesus was calling him to do. He's uncertain because he sees

things from *his* perspective only. In this moment of time, Ananias has no idea Saul would become Paul, a channel of God's blessings!

To help enlighten and thus encourage Ananias, Jesus gives some hint of what will be coming, telling Ananias to go to Saul because Saul *is*—not "going to be" but already *is*, in Jesus' eyes—His chosen instrument.

Ananias does go out in faith, finds Saul, lays hands on him, and the scales fall from his eyes. Saul, now seeing, rises and is baptized.

There may be some Ananias times in your own life, times when God calls you to do something but you hesitate. If that happens, ask God to open your eyes so you can see things from *His* perspective. Above all, trust that *He*—not you—knows the best way.

Forgive me when I hesitate, Lord, to go where You send me.
Increase my trust that You know the best way forward.

With God's perspective, I see the way forward.

Thorny Issues

*Whom have I in heaven but you? I desire you more than anything
on earth. My health may fail, and my spirit may grow weak,
but God remains the strength of my heart; he is mine forever. . . .
The Lord. . .said to me, "My grace is sufficient for you, for my power
is made perfect in weakness." . . . For the sake of Christ, then,
I am content with weaknesses, insults, hardships, persecutions,
and calamities. For when I am weak, then I am strong.*
PSALM 73:25-26 NLT; 2 CORINTHIANS 12:8-10 ESV

In his second letter to the Corinthians, the apostle Paul writes about a thorn he has in his side. He calls it "a messenger from Satan" (2 Corinthians 12:7 NLT), a malady to keep him humble. Three times he begged Jesus to remove this thorn from him. But each time, He told Paul, "I am all you need. I give you My loving-favor. My power works best in weak people" (2 Corinthians 12:9 NLV). Those words changed Paul's pattern of thinking and, in turn, transformed his attitude and life. Now, instead of pleading with God to "cure" him, Paul's finding contentment and joy in his troubles and weaknesses: "I am happy to be weak and have troubles so I can have Christ's power in me. I receive joy when I am weak" (2 Corinthians 12:9-10 NLV).

Much speculation has been made about what Paul's thorn may have been. Whether his malady was a physical, mental, spiritual, or some other kind of impediment in his life, doesn't really matter. The important thing

is that Jesus' words transformed the way Paul was looking at his life. In all probability, he was tired of the pain. He wanted his old thorn-less life back. Most likely he envied the lives of other people, ones that were in better straits than he.

You've most likely been in Paul's shoes at some point in time. You too have discovered that comparison is the key to discontentment, which is just a stone's throw from unhappiness.

Yet there is relief for you, for all God's children. No matter what your weakness, trouble, heartache, calamity, state of mind, age, or hardship, you can be content. Because Jesus is all you need. He's your true power. And it's only when you are weak that Christ's strength truly shines.

You, Jesus, are all I need in heaven and earth. Thank You for giving me the power to not just endure but be happy. Amen.

When I'm weak, God's power shines through!

Divine Guidance

You are of great worth in My eyes. You are honored
and I love you. . . . Do not fear, for I am with you. . . .
I am always with You. You hold me by my right hand.
You will lead me by telling me what I should do. . . .
Receiving an answer to their asking, they were divinely instructed
and warned in a dream not to go back to Herod; so they
departed to their own country by a different way.

Isaiah 43:4-5 nlv; Psalm 73:23-24 nlv; Matthew 2:12 ampc

When your thoughts are muddled, your loneliness at its peak, your attitude low, and feelings of being unloved on the upswing, you need some new thoughts. It's time to not just dip into but soak in God's Word.

You're very precious to God. He doesn't just love but honors you. And He's always with you—through fire, storm, flood, famine, earthquake, heartbreak, breakup, breakdown, whatever (Isaiah 43:2). He's here. By your side. So you need not fear anything or anyone. Ever.

God is also here to guide you, to help you walk Jesus' way. That means it's hand-holding time—on both sides. If you don't let go, you won't get lost. Just be sure to expect the unexpected. Because no matter what you imagine God might do, He always does something bigger and better. For the good of all.

Consider the wise men, sent for by King Herod. He was anxious to find his challenger, the newborn boy being called the King of the Jews

and, unbeknownst to the wise men, kill Him. So when the magi left to follow the prophesized star, Herod told them to let him know where they find the babe so he can "worship" Him.

The wise men followed the star and found the now two-year-old Jesus. But after they prayed for direction, God warned them not to go back to Herod. So they went home a different way. And the boy Jesus remained safe.

God has a plan. You, precious and much-loved daughter, are a part of it. And God is a part of you. Guiding you. Planning for you. Instructing you. So be a wise woman. When you need clarity, company, cheering, and cherishing, tug on the hand of your gentle King. And you will receive a transformational answer that meets your asking.

Thank You for loving, guiding, cherishing me, Lord.
Help me find my way to You. Amen.

Because God is with me, I'm divinely guided.

No Limits

There was a man named Jabez who was more honorable than any
of his brothers. His mother named him Jabez because his birth had
been so painful. He was the one who prayed to the God of Israel,
"Oh, that you would bless me and expand my territory! Please be
with me in all that I do, and keep me from all trouble
and pain!" And God granted him his request. . . .
"Whatever you ask in prayer, believe that you
have received it, and it will be yours."

1 CHRONICLES 4:9-10 NLT; MARK 11:24 ESV

Reading 1 Chronicles 1-9 can put a busy woman to sleep. It's all full of genealogies of Israel. Fathers and sons, and women every now and then, are listed ad infinitum. Yet amid these seemingly never-ending names, you find the short but fascinating account and prayer of Jabez.

A baby was born with a shadow over his entry into the world. Because his birth had been so painful for his mother, she named him Jabez, which means "pain," "oh, the pain!" (1 Chronicles 4:9 MSG), or "sorrow maker" (1 Chronicles 4:9 AMPC). Yet even with this negative appellation—even *before* his prayer—Jabez was found to be more honorable than all his brothers.

Wanting to get out from underneath the cloud of his name, the honorable Jabez decided he would not allow his birth and the pain that accompanied it to forever define his destiny and, in the process, negatively affect and limit his life. So he prayed for God's help.

Jabez asked God to bless him and to increase his property. He asked God to not just be with him in everything he did but also protect him from trouble and pain!

Jabez was a dedicated God follower who did not allow his name to become a label, a sign, a portent of who he was or would become. He did not allow himself to be either trapped or weighed down by his circumstances. Instead, he adopted a faith-filled attitude, then prayed his way out of what could have been a tortuous existence. And he was rewarded for his faith.

You can make the same decision as Jabez. To not allow thoughts about your past to define or limit your future. Instead, pray. Ask God for help. Believe you'll receive it. And you too will be rewarded for your faith.

Help me leave the past in the past, Lord.
Please bless me here and now. Amen.

Blessed in the present, I leave the past behind.

Family Ties

Ruth said. . ."Where you go I will go. . . . Your people
shall be my people, and your God my God." . . .
Judah was the father of Perez and Zerah. Their mother was
Tamar. . . . The mother of Boaz was Rahab. Boaz was the father
of Obed. The mother of Obed was Ruth. . . . King David was the
father of Solomon. His mother had been the wife of Uriah. . . .
Joseph was the husband of Mary. She was the mother of Jesus.
RUTH 1:16 ESV; MATTHEW 1:3, 5-6, 16 NLV

Although many forefathers are listed in Matthew 1's genealogy of Jesus, only five foremothers appear: Tamar, Rahab, Ruth, Bathsheba (a.k.a., the wife of Uriah in 2 Samuel 11:3), and Mary. In the first century it was very unusual to list women in a genealogy. Even more interesting is that a few of these women might not be ones you'd want included in your own family tree. Yet here they are, a good representation of those whom Jesus came to save.

Tamar, having been widowed by three brothers, posed as a prostitute to catch the eye and seed of her father-in-law Judah. Apparently, resorting to tricks and disguises was the only way she could get her father-in-law to do the right thing (Genesis 38).

Rahab, a prostitute, having heard of God's power, chose to save two of Joshua's spies. In return for her efforts, she and her family were saved in the battle of Jericho (Joshua 2, 6).

Ruth, a childless Moabite widow, traveled to Israel with her widowed mother-in-law, determined not to leave her. In return for being so loyal to Naomi, Ruth met and married Boaz.

Bathsheba, Uriah's wife, committed adultery with King David. When she became pregnant, David had her husband killed in battle, then married her. Although their first child died, Bathsheba and David went on to have Solomon (2 Samuel 11, 12).

Last but not least is the devout, blessed, and beloved virgin Mary, Jesus' mother. Describing herself as God's handmaiden, Mary is a breath of fresh air!

The point? No matter what the history of these ordinary, imperfect, and perhaps even disreputable women, they still transformed their own and the world's history by being loyal and faithful to God. They let neither their history or circumstances dictate or overshadow their lives or thinking. May you do the same.

Help me, Lord, to rise above my past and my thoughts
as I live in faithful service to You. Amen.

With God, I rise above my thoughts and circumstances.

Pliable in Ponderings

I know, GOD, that mere mortals can't run their own lives,
that men and women don't have what it takes to take
charge of life. So correct us, GOD, as you see best. . . .
John the Baptist, preaching. . .Repent (think differently; change
your mind, regretting your sins and changing your conduct). . . .
John protested strenuously, having in mind to prevent Him. . . .
But Jesus replied to him, Permit it just now; for this
is the fitting way. . . . Then he permitted Him.
JEREMIAH 10:23 MSG; MATTHEW 3:1-2, 14-15 AMPC

For thousands of years, God has been looking for men and women to turn to Him, to have a relationship with Him, to follow His course. To that end, He's gifted humankind with His Son, His Spirit, and His Book. He communicates with His people through His Word, predicaments, prayer, praise, preachers, and ordinary people. And although God followers have all these resources, there are still times when correction is needed.

John the Baptist, a testimony to the miracle-working power of God, was sent to prepare the way for the Lord Jesus. Full of the Spirit and in the power of Elijah (Luke 1:14-17), John preached in the wilderness in Judah, telling people to think differently, be sorry for their past misdeeds, and change the way they thought and acted. Wearing clothes made from camel hair and eating only locusts and honey, John began baptizing people in the Jordan River.

Then one day, Jesus came, asking John to baptize Him. But John, the Spirit-filled prophet most likely stunned by Jesus' request, tried to dissuade Him, "having in mind to prevent Him" from taking such an action. So, after much consideration, John said, "No, Jesus, I'm the one who should be baptized by *You*!" But Jesus insisted this was the right move to make. Only then did John relent and baptize Jesus.

Even when you're faithfully living your life according to God's Word, will, and way, some days you may have to change your thinking, allow your thoughts to be revised by God, doing what *He* knows is best. So allow yourself to be pliable in your ponderings, leaving the door open for God's correction and your transformation.

As I faithfully follow You and Your will, Word, and ways, Lord, help me be open to Your correction. May my ponderings be pliable.

God directs my steps in thought, word, and deed.

Unseen Footsteps

You strode right through Ocean, walked straight through roaring
Ocean, but nobody saw you come or go. Hidden in the hands of
Moses and Aaron, you led your people like a flock of sheep. . . .
Jesus was led (guided) by the [Holy] Spirit into the wilderness. . . .
As He was walking by the Sea of Galilee, He noticed two brothers. . . .
He said to them, Come after Me [as disciples—letting Me be
your Guide], follow Me, and I will make you fishers of men! . . .
And great crowds joined and accompanied Him.
PSALM 77:19-20 MSG; MATTHEW 4:1, 18-19, 25 AMPC

Whether you're going through dire straits or merely performing daily duties, there is only one safe course for you: following, submitting to, and remaining true to your Lord and Savior.

When the Israelites were being pursued by an army behind them while surrounded on both sides by walls of seawater, God led them safely through—the only possible way out of their predicament. It was the Lord's power that held the water back, His power that—though unseen, invisible, untraceable—enabled His people to stay the course, survive, and later thrive.

It was God's Spirit who led the Messiah into the wilderness where He fasted for forty days and forty nights, then met and overcame the challenges of Satan. It was God's Son, Jesus, who noticed some fishermen, called them to Him, and became their guide, transforming them into

disciples, fishers, and leaders of men and women.

God's power is vast. His penchant for transforming His people broad. His ways, guidance, and empowerment, at times, beyond understanding, invisible, untraceable, unseen—but there, ready and waiting to help you.

So when you're not sure which way to go or where God is, when you're uncertain of what lies ahead, beside, or before you, remember what He has done for His people in the past. Reflect upon how He puts shepherds in your life to lend you His hand. Know that although you may not be able to see God, He is with you, guiding you, working within you to develop, empower, and transform you into the woman you were made to be in thought, word, and deed.

Lord, with You taking care of me in so many seen and unseen ways, I feel so blessed. With You in my life, I know that all is and will be well with my soul. Lead on, Lord. Lead on. Amen.

God is my strength and guide.

God-Confidence

*You shall [earnestly] remember all the way which the Lord your
God led you these forty years in the wilderness, to humble you and
to prove you, to know what was in your [mind and] heart,
whether you would keep His commandments or not. . . .
Don't be so naive and self-confident. You're not exempt. You could
fall flat on your face as easily as anyone else. Forget about
self-confidence; it's useless. Cultivate God-confidence.*

DEUTERONOMY 8:2 AMPC; 1 CORINTHIANS 10:12 MSG

*I'm weak. . . . I'm worthless. . . . I can never do anything right. . . . No one
loves me. . . .* Thoughts such as these are easy to identify as negative,
harmful to yourself. It's safe to say God hates such inner dialogue. But
there are some other thoughts that, while they may not sound "negative"
to you, are *definitely* negative to God. Thoughts that go something like
this: *Am I awesome or what? I am so proud of myself for earning all this
money! And all on my own too!* Or, *It's because I'm so right and good that
God has blessed me.* These pride-filled thoughts can definitely lead to
negative consequences.

The Israelites' trek through the wilderness was a trial, a test of what
God's people were made of, what they were thinking in their hearts and
minds. He wanted to see if they would follow Him, listen to Him, give
credit where credit was due.

God's desire was to help His children. But once they *were* helped,

He didn't want them thinking it was all their own doing. In Deuteronomy, God tells the people, "If you start thinking to yourselves, 'I did all this. And all by myself. I'm rich. It's all mine!'—well, think again. Remember that GOD, your God, gave you the strength to produce all this wealth so as to confirm the covenant that he promised to your ancestors" (8:17-18 MSG).

In Deuteronomy 9:4, God warns His people about thinking, "'It's because of all the good I've done that GOD has brought me in here to dispossess these nations.' Actually it's because of all the evil these nations have done" (MSG).

In other words, for your good and God's, give prideful thoughts the door. "Forget about self-confidence. . . . Cultivate God-confidence"!

Help me stay humble and grateful, remembering that all I have comes from You, Lord— regardless of the amount of effort I expend or how "good" I may think I am. Amen.

All the good I am and have comes from God's hands.

Power, Promises, Presence

"Perhaps you will think to yourselves, 'How can we ever conquer these nations that are so much more powerful than we are?' But don't be afraid of them! Just remember what the LORD your God did. . . . Remember the miraculous signs and wonders, and the strong hand and powerful arm with which he brought you out of Egypt. The LORD your God will use this same power against all the people you fear." . . . Jesus came and touched them and said, Get up, and do not be afraid.

DEUTERONOMY 7:17-19 NLT; MATTHEW 17:7 AMPC

In Deuteronomy 7:17-19, God tells the Israelites not to think thoughts of fear, not to speak them into their hearts and minds. He tells His people not to shake in their sandals when they come up against powerful nations. Instead, they're to remember—in detail—what God did to Pharaoh and all of Egypt.

God's people were witnesses to all the plagues He'd brought. They saw the signs, wonders, and miracles His servants Moses and Aaron preformed, how He used His mighty hand and His outstretched arm to aid their escape, holding back the walls of the Red Sea while shrouding His people with His cloud, putting Himself between them and their enemy.

Finally, God tells His people that all those things He did against Egypt and its king He will do for them against all other peoples they may fear. God then commands them, *"You will not be afraid of them. For the Lord your God is among you, a great and powerful God"*

(Deuteronomy 7:21 NLV, emphasis added).

Why is God doing all this? Because He loves His people, because He keeps His promises (Deuteronomy 7:8-9).

What does God want His people, including you, to do when fear awakens within? To remember who God is and what He has done (in detail). To remember there is no other God but Him (Deuteronomy 4:39). To remember to "love the Lord God with all your [mind and] heart and with your entire being and with all your might" and to keep His commandments "[first] in your [own] minds and heart" (Deuteronomy 6:5-6 AMPC).

Today, allow God to help you renew your mind by replacing your thoughts of fear with His power, promises, and presence.

I'm tired of living in fear, Lord. When I start to shake in my shoes, prompt me to remember You, Your love, Your power, Your Promises, and Your presence. In Jesus' name I pray, amen.

Thoughts of God's power, promises, and presence dispel my fear.

A Lost Art

*I will listen [with expectancy] to what God the Lord
will say, for He will speak peace to His people. . . .
They shall not be put to shame who wait for,
look for, hope for, and expect Me. . . .
Behold, I stand at the door and knock; if anyone hears
and listens to and heeds My voice and opens the door, I will
come in to him and will eat with him, and he [will eat] with Me.*
PSALM 85:8; ISAIAH 49:23; REVELATION 3:20 AMPC

Listening has almost become a lost art. We're too eager, wanting to get our next words out, to get our point across, to pay any attention to what another person is saying. At times we don't even let someone finish his or her sentence before we're diving right back in to what may no longer be a conversation but a diatribe or a monologue. And. . .it may just be that we're treating our conversations with God the same way.

Prayer is a two-way street. There is a time to get things out, to ask questions, to confess, to unload your biggest burdens. That's your part. And as you talk, God, at the other end of the line, is listening, with all His mind, soul, and heart.

When you've finished, it's time for God to talk. Not a time for you to put words in His mouth, think about your next question or complaint, fall asleep, or get up and walk away. This is your turn to listen attentively and expect an answer. To have Him speak peace to your heart. To wait

for, look for, hope for, and expect God to not just be there but answer.

Keep this in mind every time you pray. For the path to transformation is made up by moments in which you've allowed God to speak, through His Word or prayer. When you've allowed God to exchange your thoughts with His.

Today, as you go to the Word and into prayer, remember that Jesus is knocking at your door. So let all distractions fade away. Then, when you *hear* Jesus knocking, actually *listen to* and heed His voice. Open wide your door so He can come in and commune with you.

Help me, Lord, to relearn the art of listening, beginning with my time with You. As I come to prayer, Jesus, quiet my mind. Rid me of all distractions. For I'm longing to hear You knock, to have a heart-to-heart, ear-to-ear communion with You. Amen.

When Jesus knocks, I listen with expectancy.

Centering

*When I am afraid, I will put my trust in you. I praise God
for what he has promised. I trust in God, so why should
I be afraid? What can mere mortals do to me? . . .
We can say with confidence, "The LORD is my helper,
so I will have no fear. What can mere people do to me?"*

PSALM 56:3-4; HEBREWS 13:6 NLT

One of the biggest things that trips up our thoughts is fear. Fear of anyone and everything that threatens us or those we love. What's worse is that it doesn't seem to matter whether that fear is imaginary or justifiable. Either way, when it creeps into our lives, our built-in, automatic fight-flight-freeze response kicks in. And off we go, into the wild blue yonder of fearful and fretful thoughts.

David, the apple of God's eye, often became afraid. Yet he was also aware of his fear triggers and alert to his reactions. He knew where to go when trouble came knocking—to God. The Being who'd seen David at his worst, keeping track of his concerns, his tears, his ups and downs (Psalm 56:8). Just as God had not ignored David's concerns in the past, He will not ignore them now. And God, bigger than any foes or fears David was up against, would know exactly what David would need and when.

Psalm 56 was written when David was taken captive by the Philistines and his fear understandably kicks in. After all, David had killed their Goliath, as well as many other Philistines. They'd probably been itching

to kill him for ages.

Yet instead of giving in to fear, David sets His eyes on God, centering on the Lord who'd saved him time and time again. David admits his fear yet goes right for the remedy: "When I am afraid, I will put my trust in You." Having put his trust in God, he can now turn it around, saying to himself, "I trust in God, so why should I be afraid? What can mere mortals do to me?"

Like David, you are the apple in the eye of a God who loves and looks out *for* you. He alone is your helper. So have no fear-filled thoughts or worries. People and circumstances have no power over you when you trust in God!

Lord, so often my fears get the better of my thoughts. Help me turn things around. As I trust in and focus on You, my fears fade while You and Your power grow! Amen.

Because I trust in God, I am not afraid.

The Caretaker

"I tell prisoners, 'Come on out. You're free!' and those huddled in fear,
'It's all right. It's safe now.' There'll be foodstands along all the roads,
picnics on all the hills—nobody hungry, nobody thirsty, shade from
the sun, shelter from the wind, for the Compassionate One
guides them, takes them to the best springs." . . .
You can be sure that God will take care
of everything you need.
ISAIAH 49:9-10; PHILIPPIANS 4:19 MSG

Some days you just want someone to tell you, "It's all right. It's safe now. You're okay. I'm going to take care of everything you need." And that's fine. It's normal to need and seek reassurance that all will be well, that you'll be taken care of no matter how bad things may look or seem. Yet this needing and seeking of comfort can backfire—if you look to the wrong source.

Looking for caretaking from another human, possessions, or substance usually has dismal results. The fact is humans aren't perfect by any stretch of the imagination. So the chances of them always coming through for you are slim. Finding comfort in possessions won't fit the bill either. For although a new dress may provide solace today, it probably won't next month. Finding your needs met via substances is the most dangerous avenue to take. Today's opioid epidemic is the perfect example of how that remedy is no remedy.

If you need anything, no matter how great or trivial, God wants you to come to Him. If you're addicted to, chained to, or imprisoned, God is telling you that you are free. If you're full of fear, God is telling you that you are safe. Everything you need is provided by His hand. In Him, you'll not want for water or food. If you follow Him, He'll guide you exactly where you need to go, giving you what you need to live, breathe, and thrive.

God does not want you to have a mind-set of lack. To worry about where you might find your next meal or bed. To be anxious about where you might find a job. To fret over the coming medical fee, tax bill, or mortgage payment.

Woman, change your mind-set. Know God will provide, take care of, be the source of everything you could possibly need, as you look to and walk with Him on this side of heaven.

Lord, help me let go of this idea of lack in my life.
Today, I reach out to You instead, knowing You are
the Source and supplier of all I need. Amen.

In God, I am safe, calm, loved, and cared for.

Choose

"I have set before you life and death,
the blessings and the curses; therefore choose life.". . .
"If you think it is wrong to serve the Lord,
choose today whom you will serve." . . .
Let's not get tired of doing what is good. At just the right
time we will reap a harvest of blessing if we don't give up.
DEUTERONOMY 30:19 AMPC; JOSHUA 24:15 NLV; GALATIANS 6:9 NLT

Every moment of every day you have a myriad of decisions to make. You can choose life or death, blessings or curses, God or idols, doing good or giving up. Intermingled within these choices is which thoughts you'll let linger in your mind: positive or negative.

The positive thoughts are aligned with God's, leading you to live the life He wants you to live, a life of blessings, serving Him, and doing good. The negative thoughts are aligned with worldly thoughts, leading toward lifelessness, curses, serving other gods, and giving up even looking for good things.

Amazing power comes from having positive thoughts. For positive thoughts shared aloud encourage others, bringing the best out of them, changing their moods, and in the process, the world.

Gene Kranz was flight director when the Apollo 13 crew experienced an onboard explosion. Their lives hung in the balance as pandemonium erupted at mission control. To get the men's minds on the matter at hand,

Gene spoke through the chaos, saying positive things like, "Let's look at this thing from a standpoint of status. What've we got on the spacecraft that's good?" "Failure is not an option." "I don't care about what anything was designed to do. I care about what it can do."

After getting the best out of the men on earth and in space, the time came for the Apollo 13 crew to reenter earth's atmosphere. That's when NASA's Chris Kraft said, "This could be the worst disaster NASA's ever faced." Kranz's response was, "With all due respect, sir, I believe this is going to be our finest hour."

Your thoughts matter—for they shape the words you share with yourself, God, and others. They also bring you life or death, blessings or curses.

Today, vow to serve God by becoming aware of your thoughts and changing them up when needed, realigning them so they agree with what God would have you think and believe. And you'll find yourself reaping a harvest of blessings—for yourself and others.

Lord, help me keep my thoughts aligned with Yours. Amen.

Today I choose to think positive thoughts.

No Second-Guessing

"Every promise of God proves true; he protects everyone who runs to him for help. So don't second-guess him."...
Who in the world do you think you are to second-guess God? Do you for one moment suppose any of us knows enough to call God into question?...
God can do anything, you know—far more than you could ever imagine or guess or request in your wildest dreams! He does it not by pushing us around but by working within us.

PROVERBS 30:5-6; ROMANS 9:20; EPHESIANS 3:20 MSG

How many times have your thoughts led you astray as you tried to guess what was going to happen next? Then, based on that guess and its accompanying assumptions, you began taking actions that led you away from God and His will for you, creating a major mess in the process, an entanglement that only God could eventually straighten out.

Back to the Apollo 13 story. . . . After the spacecraft suffered an onboard explosion, NASA begins trying to figure out how it can get the three astronauts back safely to earth. With all that kept going wrong, NASA's goal seemed impossible. Flight director Gene Kranz's advice to mission control was, "Let's work the problem people. Let's not make things worse by guessing." That's good advice for any problem-solving.

Jim Lovell, the captain of the Apollo 13 crew, was having his own problems in space. Astronaut Jack Swigert was panicking. He'd begun

assuming mission control didn't have a reentry plan. That the spacecraft was coming in too shallow, too fast. He figured they wouldn't have enough power to get home. And on and on and on.

Finally, Jim Lovell told him, "Now listen, there's a thousand things that have to happen in order. We are on number eight. You're talking about number 692."

Lovell could be calm because he'd faced a crisis before. While in flight during combat, everything goes dark in his cockpit. Instruments, homing signal, and lights are gone. Suddenly he sees a trail of phosphorescent algae churned up by the carrier he'd been looking for. He concludes, "You never know. . .what events are going to transpire to get you home."

Forget about second-guessing God. Don't panic. Remember that He can do anything. Beyond what you could ever guess, dream, or imagine. So keep your thoughts firmly rooted in His promises, knowing He'll lead you safely home.

Help me, Lord, to trust in Your promises, not my assumptions. Amen.

I trust in God's promises—not my guesses!

Looking Up

I delivered you; I answered you in the secret
place. . . . Open your mouth wide and I will fill it. . . .
I carry you. I have made, and I will bear; yes, I will carry and will save
you. . . . Bring it again to mind and lay it to heart. . . . I am God. . . .
"Things are looking up! . . . Last night God's angel stood at my side. . .
saying to me, 'Don't give up, Paul. You're going to stand before
Caesar yet—and everyone sailing with you is also going to make it.'"
PSALM 81:7, 10 AMPC; ISAIAH 46:4, 8-9 AMPC; ACTS 27:22-24 MSG

No matter what your thoughts may lead you to believe, God's ears, eyes, and heart are open to your voice, visions, and sorrows. When you call out to Him, He will not just answer you but deliver you. And He will nourish you with whatever you need. He promises that if you will just open your mouth, He will feed you!

This same God has not just made you, then discarded you, left you on the side of the road. No, ma'am! Your Creator loves you, continues to mold you, and is ready, willing, and able to carry you—that's His promise! No matter how old or how young you are. Through storm, heartache, hurricane, strike, famine, flu, you name it. God is going to bear you, put you on His shoulders, taking you wherever you need to go. Remember these things. Get them straight in your mind and heart.

God not only protects, carries, provides for, and answers you. He's also placed angels over you. They stand by you to protect you, to give

you hope, to encourage you. They take care of you whenever you need them, wherever you are.

God tells you these truths over and over again. Your job is to believe them. To saturate yourself in God's Word so that when erroneous thoughts creep into your mind, you'll become immediately unsettled, leading you to set His Word against them. Then, once you've realigned your thinking, matching it to your Lord's, you'll once more be walking in rhythm with God, living in His truth.

Thank You, Lord, for loving me, holding me, carrying me, bearing me. Thank You for placing me in the care of Your angels. I'm looking up to You! In You alone I trust and believe! Amen.

Things are looking up as God's promises are coming true in my life.

Thought Watchers

Whoever trusts in his own mind is a fool,
but he who walks in wisdom will be delivered. . . .
We break down every thought and proud thing that puts
itself up against the wisdom of God. We take hold
of every thought and make it obey Christ.

PROVERBS 28:26 ESV; 2 CORINTHIANS 10:5 NLV

In the 2011 Margaret Thatcher biopic, *The Iron Lady*, Meryl Streep, speaking as Thatcher, said, "Watch your thoughts, for they become words. Watch your words, for they become actions. Watch your actions for they become habits. Watch your habits, for they become your character. And watch your character, for it becomes your destiny. What we think, we become." Those are powerful words. Yet they seem to leave one hanging, wondering about that powerful and initial catalyst: *"Watch your thoughts."*

Proverbs doesn't tell us *how* to watch our thoughts but does tell us not to trust them. If we do, we'll look like a fool. On the other hand, if we walk by the wisdom we find in God's Word, we'll be saved. Whew! That's a close one!

Second Corinthians 10:5 gives us more thoughtful advice. There we see we're to destroy any arguments or opinions that go against the wisdom in God's Word. Simply "take hold of every thought and make it obey Christ."

Yet what does *that* mean practically, on a minute-by-minute basis?

That's a very important question, considering we think 50,000 to 70,000 thoughts per day—and that 80 percent of those are negative!

To take hold of thoughts and make them obey Christ, you must first find time to be still before God. You must admit to Him (and yourself) that you're responsible for what you're thinking. Then ask Him to help you sort out your thoughts. Turn over any thoughts that are really crippling your life or walk with Christ. Then change any other thoughts that need to be better aligned with God's.

The more you ask God to help you with your thoughts, the better you'll be at thought watching. And the better you are at thought watching, the more you'll find yourself choosing good things to feed your brain (Philippians 4:8).

As you practice watching your thoughts, know that God is helping you. And with His support, you *will* succeed in thinking thoughts that lead to right words, actions, habits, character, and destiny.

Lord, help me capture my thoughts, making them amenable to You and Your Word. Amen.

With God's help, I'm regaining control of my thoughts.

The New You

*Awake, awake, put on your strength. . . . For you will not go
out with haste, nor will you go in flight. . .for the Lord will go
before you, and the God of Israel will be your rear guard. . . .
Be constantly renewed in the spirit of your mind. . .and put on
the new nature (the regenerate self) created in God's image. . . .
Go; it shall be done for you as you have believed.*
ISAIAH 52:1, 12; EPHESIANS 4:23-24; MATTHEW 8:13 AMPC

Today is your day. This is when you awaken to who you are in Christ.
Today you'll put on your strength and live as the woman God says you are.

God wants you to leave your old life behind. To let go of a mind-set
that had you enslaved, feeling powerless and hopeless. But you need not
be afraid of the new you. Because God is walking before you, leading you
to new pastures. He also walks behind you, guarding you from the rear.

But first, you must "Strip yourselves of your former nature [put off
and discard your old unrenewed self] which characterized your previous
manner of life and becomes corrupt through lusts *and* desires that spring
from delusion" (Ephesians 4:22 AMPC). Your previous self was that old
woman who had your former mind-set. The one who saw all the flaws
in her life and self and others. The woman with a heart weighed down
by trouble, a soul burdened by bitterness, a mind more focused on bad
news than the Good News. She's the lady who followed her delusions,
imaginings, and assumptions more than God's wisdom.

After throwing off that old you, endeavor to "be constantly renewed in the spirit of your mind [having a fresh mental and spiritual attitude]" (Ephesians 4:23 AMPC). Soak yourself in the Word, daily looking for truths to give you peace, strength, and power. As you become more and more aware of your thoughts, bring them before Jesus, allowing Him to help you rework and reword them, so your mind-set will become more and more like His.

Then finally, in the power of your faith, put on the new you. Live as the woman God created you to be. And "Go. What you believed could happen has happened" (Matthew 6:13 MSG)!

---

*Thank You for awakening me to the possibilities in You, Lord.
Today I put on the new me! Amen.*

As I yield my thoughts to the Spirit, I'm remade in God's image!

Good Reports

The other men who had explored the land with him disagreed.
"We can't go up against them! They are stronger than we are!"
So they spread this bad report. . . . Then the whole
community began weeping. . . .
They did know God, but they did not honor Him as God.
They were not thankful to Him and thought only of foolish
things. Their foolish minds became dark. They said that
they were wise, but they showed how foolish they were.

<small>NUMBERS 13:31-32; 14:1 NLT; ROMANS 1:21-22 NLV</small>

It's the end of what, in *your* mind, has been a long, terrible day. When you finally arrive home, someone asks you, "How was your day?" What a loaded question!

After heaving a long sigh, you begin reciting everything that'd gone wrong for you, replaying each in your mind while doing so. First, you relate how your day got off to a late start because you missed the exit, got off at the wrong station, or spilled your coffee all over your clothes. Then the copier broke down, the boss chewed you out, the report arrived late, the baby threw up. You go on and on. When you finally take a breath, your listener interrupts, "Okay. Now, tell me something *good* that happened today."

You're stunned. Your negative thoughts pull back, allowing you to reconsider the day's happenings. A light begins to dawn upon your

mind. Slowly, more carefully, you begin talking about a driver who let you go before him at a four-way stop. Oh, and an old friend called you, right out of the blue! And you found a quarter in the grocery parking lot! Suddenly, you realize your day seems to have been pretty good after all!

After Moses sent twelve spies into the Promised Land, ten came back with a bad report, saying the people who lived there were giants. There's no way they could go up against them. But Caleb and Joshua had a different story: with God on their side, they could defeat anyone and anything. Yet it was the bad story that circulated and spread distrust of God.

The Lord had wanted His people to focus on the *goodness* of the land, not the strength of the people who lived there. It's the same with you. God wants you focused on the good things you experience (including Him)—not on the power of forces against you.

Lord, I'm only focusing on, thinking about, and reporting on the good things—and leaving the not-so-good in Your hands! Amen!

With God, only good things happen!

Mind Reader

"Know the God of your father. Serve Him with a whole heart and a willing mind. For the Lord looks into all hearts, and understands every plan and thought. If you look to Him, He will let you find Him."...
At once Jesus knew the teachers of the Law were thinking this. He said to them, "Why do you think this in your hearts? Which is easier to say to the sick man, 'Your sins are forgiven,' or to say, 'Get up, take your bed, and start to walk?' "

1 CHRONICLES 28:9; MARK 2:8-9 NLV

Jesus knows exactly what you're thinking—even those ideas, beliefs, and plans you hold deep within your heart and mind.

Jesus was teaching at a believer's house. The place was packed! So there was no room for the four men who came carrying a paralyzed man on a stretcher. Realizing they couldn't reach Jesus because of the crowd, the men dug a hole in the roof and lowered the man down through it.

Jesus, seeing their faith and confidence in the powers of God, was impressed. So He said to the paralyzed man, "Your sins are forgiven."

This statement confounded the teachers of the Law. They began thinking in their hearts, "Why does this Man talk like this? He is speaking as if He is God! Who can forgive sins? Only One can forgive sins and that is God!" (Mark 2:7 NLV). Hearing their thoughts, Jesus repeated them back to the silent thinkers in question form. Then, desiring to prove that He had not just the power to forgive sins but to heal, Jesus told the

paralyzed man to get up and go home. And he did—amazing one and all!

There is no secret, plan, thought, or motive you can hide from God. Even your simple musings reach God's ears.

Today might be time for a heart and mind check. For you to ask God if there's any thought or motive within you that needs to be questioned by Him. If there is, ask Him to help you understand, then to realign your thoughts to match His or discard them altogether.

"Create in me a clean heart, O God, and renew a right spirit within me"
(Psalm 51:10 ESV). Help me realign my thoughts where needed,
so that they're closer to Yours. Give me the wisdom
I need in thought, word, and deed. Amen.

God renews my heart, mind, and spirit.

Lifted Up

In the day of trouble He will keep me safe in His holy tent.
In the secret place of His tent He will hide me. He will set
me high upon a rock. Then my head will be lifted up. . . .
Don't shuffle along, eyes to the ground, absorbed with the things
right in front of you. Look up, and be alert to what is going on around
Christ—that's where the action is. See things from his perspective.
Your old life is dead. Your new life, which is your real life—
even though invisible to spectators—is with Christ in God.

PSALM 27:5-6 NLV; COLOSSIANS 3:2-3 MSG

It seems so easy to get so absorbed, so drawn into the material world that you stop opening up to Christ—in heart, mind, and soul. You stop looking for areas in which He may be calling you. Instead, you get wrapped up in the day-to-day grind, working for that next paycheck so that you can cover the tax bill, get groceries, pay the rent, and wake up the next day just to do it all over again.

Yet that's not why God put you here on earth. He wants you to look up. To see the sky, birds, trees, clouds, sun, and moon and be reminded of Him. To think about heaven and God, His powers, forgiveness, blessings, Son—all the good things unobtainable on earth. To remember that you're to love Him with all your mind, strength, heart, and soul, and love your neighbors as yourself.

For when you're mindful of God and heaven, when you recall what

He'd have you be and do, that's when you begin to see Him, yourself, and others, from *His* perspective. That's a life changer!

You, as a believer, are to be living a life hidden with Christ in God. That's how you're kept in His hands, safe in His secret place, high upon a rock. There you'll find the quiet you need to revamp your thinking, the security you cannot acquire on earth. That's where God can get a good grip on you, so He can hold you above all the things in this earth that try to pull you down.

Lord, lift me up to the high rock, that secret place within You, a place of peace, safety, stillness way above the world. For I know it's there I'll find that mind-altering joy and perspective I crave. Amen.

Setting my mind on things above, I find new life!

Clarity in Conversation

"This is GOD's Message, the God who made earth, made it livable and lasting, known everywhere as GOD: 'Call to me and I will answer you. I'll tell you marvelous and wondrous things that you could never figure out on your own.'" . . .
In the middle of their talk and questions, Jesus came up and walked along with them. But they were not able to recognize who he was. . . . Then he started at the beginning, with the Books of Moses, and went on through all the Prophets, pointing out everything in the Scriptures that referred to him.

JEREMIAH 33:2-3; LUKE 24:15-16, 27 MSG

You can talk with other believers until your face is blue, but there are just some things you and they may not understand without God's help, without His insights, revelations, and wisdom to help you.

After Jesus' resurrection, two of His followers were walking on the road to Emmaus. On the way, they talked about all the events that had happened since Jesus' death and burial. Next thing they knew, someone had joined them. It was Jesus, but for some reason His identity remained hidden from them.

As they walked along, Jesus asked what they'd been discussing so intently. So they told Him all the events that had transpired concerning Jesus of Nazareth. Toward the end of their story, they said, "Some of our women have completely confused us" (Luke 24:22 MSG). Apparently, they'd

gone to Jesus' tomb. He wasn't there but some angels were—and they said Jesus was alive! But when some of the men went to check, the tomb was empty and Jesus nowhere to be found.

Jesus told the two men how "thick-headed" and "slow-hearted" they were! Then He went on to explain everything to them.

Sometimes your very conversations with others or within yourself are like a call to God. He sees the direction your thoughts are heading and wants to set you straight.

On those days when you need clarity, call out to God. Listen for His voice. Be patient, waiting expectantly for Him to appear by your side as you walk, wait, work, wake, or wander. Know that God will keep His promise to tell you everything you can't figure out on your own and so much more!

Oh Jesus, sometimes I'm just plain confused. So I'm calling on You.
Bring me understanding, Lord. Tell me marvelous things
I could never figure out without Your help. Amen.

When I call, God gives me clarity!

Powered by the Rock

"Give ear, O heavens, and I will speak, and let the earth hear the words of my mouth. May my teaching drop as the rain, my speech distill as the dew, like gentle rain upon the tender grass, and like showers upon the herb. For I will proclaim the name of the LORD; ascribe greatness to our God! The Rock, his work is perfect." . . . We can say these things because of our faith in God through Christ. We know we are not able in ourselves to do any of this work. God makes us able to do these things.

DEUTERONOMY 32:1-4 ESV; 2 CORINTHIANS 3:4-5 NLV

When you have self-defeating thoughts, ones that rule out any help and power from God, take a good look at what God did for Moses.

Moses was a Hebrew boy raised by the princess of Egypt. But he never forgot his people. As a grown-up, he witnessed a fellow Hebrew being beaten by an Egyptian. So Moses killed and then buried the Egyptian in the sand. When word of his actions spread, Moses ran away to Midian.

It was there, forty years later, that God spoke to Moses from a burning bush, telling him to free His people from slavery in Egypt.

Moses asked Him, "Why me?"

God replied, "You'll be fine. I'll be with you."

Moses then asked, "What if they ask who sent me?"

God said, "Just tell them the I AM WHO I AM sent you."

Then Moses asked, "What can I do to prove You sent me?" So God

demonstrated some miracles using Moses' rod and skin.

Finally, Moses told God he stammers. God, now a bit angry, told Moses to get going. He'll be with him, telling him what to say. And He'll send his brother Aaron along, to be used as needed.

Moses had come a long way by the time he's singing with such poetic eloquence in Deuteronomy 32. And just as God worked through Moses, He can work through you, enabling you to do the work to which you've been called. For if God can gift the somewhat rebellious and imperfect Moses, He can surely gift you.

With You empowering me and walking with me, Lord, I know I can do what You've called me to do. Please help me let go of any self-doubts as I step up in You. In Jesus' name, amen!

I can do anything when God walks with me.

Permanent Font

Though the mountains should depart and the hills be shaken or removed, yet My love and kindness shall not depart from you, nor shall My covenant of peace and completeness be removed, says the Lord, Who has compassion on you. . . . Who can keep us away from the love of Christ? Can trouble or problems? Can suffering wrong from others or having no food? Can it be because of no clothes or because of danger or war? . . . For I know that nothing can keep us from the love of God. . .which is ours through Christ Jesus our Lord.

ISAIAH 54:10 AMPC; ROMANS 8:35, 38-39 NLV

Human love can be fickle. Sometimes you just can't count on the compassion of another person. So, thank God for God! For His love for you, His compassion for you can never be shaken, loosed, removed. Even if everything else in your life is falling apart, knowing that God's love and kindness will always be there for you is an amazing anchor for your soul, a stabilizer for your mind, and a balm for your emotions.

Yet it's not just God's love, compassion, and kindness you can always count on. It's also the peace He brings you, the sense of completeness you feel when you're in His presence. This too is something that can never be taken away from you.

Romans 8:38-39 gives you an even longer list of things that cannot, by any stretch of your imagination, come between you and your Lord.

So if you've been thinking that death, life, angels, leaders, and any other powers have kept you from God's love, think again! Not even "hard things now or in the future" (Romans 8:38 NLV) can separate you from God's love. Nor anything in the world above or below—or any other living thing!

Yet to live a life secured by God's love takes faith. Lots of it. You have to believe that even when you have "trouble or calamity, or are persecuted or hungry, or destitute, or in danger, or threatened with death. . .despite all these things, overwhelming victory" (Romans 8:35, 37 NLT) is yours through Christ who loves you.

Today, tap into God's never-ending, permanent font of love, kindness, peace, compassion, and wholeness that's waiting just for you. Know that no matter what happens in your life, nothing can keep you from God's immense love.

Thank You, Lord, for Your love for me, a love that has no end. Amen.

God's love for me will never be shaken.

Woman, Be Happy

"Fill the air with song. . . . Clear lots of ground for your tents! Make your tents large. Spread out! Think big! Use plenty of rope, drive the tent pegs deep. . . . Don't be afraid—you're not going to be embarrassed. Don't hold back—you're not going to come up short. . . . You'll be built solid, grounded in righteousness, far from any trouble—nothing to fear! . . . If any should attack, nothing will come of it. . . . This is what GOD's servants can expect. I'll see to it that everything works out for the best." . . . God makes all things work together for the good of those who love Him.

ISAIAH 54:1-2, 4, 14-15, 17 MSG; ROMANS 8:28 NLV

Past treatment and experiences, as well as your current circumstances and thoughts, may keep you fearful, discouraging you from stepping into the life God has waiting for you. But, if you're ready, God is going to help you turn your life around by getting you in the right frame of mind.

When you want and need to be lifted high—way above your doubts, fears, discouragements, reservations, and troubles—immerse yourself in Isaiah 54. Once you begin reading its first words, "Woman, be happy. . . . Cry for joy" (NLV), you'll find there's no turning back!

Speaking through the prophet Isaiah, God tells you not to be afraid, because you won't be embarrassed. Nor to hold back on anything, because you'll never lack for anything—especially God's love for you (Isaiah 54:10).

God also promises you a firm foundation. As you ground your life in Him, you'll be far from any trouble. Best of all, you'll have "nothing to fear!" Because if you get attacked, "nothing will come of it."

Why is God doing all this? Because He's not just your Maker. He's also your Husband. This relationship you're in with the Lord of the universe is not some long-distance romance. It's a commitment to a supernatural being, a marriage of spirits filled with joy and passion.

To continually keep your head in the right place, your thoughts on the heavenly side, sink your mind into Isaiah 54 at *least* once a week. Read it slowly, allowing it to penetrate all aspects of your being. As you do so, God and His Word will transform you. Ready? Set? Grow!

I'm ready, Lord! Help me get into the right frame of mind! Amen.

In God, I find my joy and song.

Calm Amid the Storm

The Lord knows the thoughts of man, that they are vain
(empty and futile—only a breath). Blessed (happy, fortunate,
to be envied) is the man whom You discipline and instruct, O Lord,
and teach out of Your law, that You may give him power
to keep himself calm in the days of adversity. . . .
There arose a violent storm on the sea, so that the boat was
being covered up by the waves; but He was sleeping. . . .
Then He got up and rebuked the winds and the sea, and there
was a great and wonderful calm (a perfect peaceableness).
PSALM 94:11-13 AMPC; MATTHEW 8:24, 26 AMPC

God knows what you're thinking. Always has. Always will. He also knows some of your thoughts can be shallow, brief, and empty compared to His. That's why He is so eager to change things up, to help you renew your mind.

Yet for God to turn your mind to His way of thinking, you must allow Him to teach you. You must be open to His concepts, even if you don't comprehend them. To admit God and His Word are right—even if you have a good argument for your side.

As you become more and more teachable, you'll find God has empowered you to stay calm amid the chaos! You'll be confident that when you find yourself slipping, God will be there to catch you, lift you up, support you with His undying love. When your anxious thoughts and

doubts begin multiplying within your mind, you'll find God's comfort bringing you "renewed hope and cheer" (Psalm 94:19 NLT).

Never be in doubt that God is alert and waiting for your call. That even during the most violent storms, He's with you. And because He's with you, there's no need for you to have a fearful mind-set. For His Son, Jesus, is not just Lord of your life, He's Lord of the earth. The winds and waves pounding against you, leading you to think you're bound to sink, are under His complete control. Just call on Him. Then await the "great and wonderful calm (a perfect peaceableness)" to roll over you and lead you safely to shore.

Lord, I know Your thoughts and wisdom are so much higher than my own. So please make me more teachable, so I can gain the power of calm amid the storm.

God has empowered me to be calm amid the storm.

Power of Union

"The Lord says to you, 'Do not be afraid or troubled. . . . Just stand still
in your places and see the saving power of the Lord work for you.'
. . . Trust in the Lord your God, and you will be made strong." . . .
In conclusion, be strong in the Lord [be empowered through your
union with Him]; draw your strength from Him [that strength
which His boundless might provides]. Put on God's whole
armor. . .that you may be able successfully to stand.
2 CHRONICLES 20:15, 17, 20 NLV; EPHESIANS 6:10-11 AMPC

Your transformation under God's hands is an ever-widening and exhilarating road. There will be ups and downs. A few steps forward sometimes followed by a few steps back. But God's major message to you throughout this whole process of transforming your life and mind is to not be afraid. Don't worry about anything. Just surrender yourself. Be still as God ministers to you, reshapes you, and works in, with, through, and for you.

Yet God knows you may find it difficult to surrender yourself to Him. That's where trust plays a big part. To help you increase your faith and knowledge of who God is, how much He wants and plans good for you, take up this final challenge.

Find a Bible translation that really speaks to your heart. Vow to read it from beginning to end—no matter how long it takes. Find a Bible-reading plan you'd like to follow. Or read three chapters a day: one from the Old

Testament, one from the New, and one from the Psalms. Before reading, pray, saying something like, "Speak, Lord. Your servant is listening" (1 Samuel 3:10).

In each chapter you read, underline one or more Bible verses that lift your spirit and speak to your soul. Take them to God. Allow His voice to calm, strengthen, and inspire you, drawing you ever close to Him. Ask the Lord to apply His message to your heart. Then carry His words with you throughout the day.

As you continue to surrender yourself to God, allow your union with Him to provide you with the strength and energy you need to follow Him. And bit by bit, you, God's woman of wonder, will be transformed. So that you can one day stand before Him, surrounded by His love and heavenly light, hearing His voice say, "Welcome home, daughter."

Speak, Lord. I'm listening. Amen.

My union with God empowers me.

Topical Index

Looking for immediate guidance and power to help you shore up your faith? In this index you will find a list of emotions, feelings, or mind-sets that will guide you to the encouragement you need within God's precious Word for you, for life.

Abandonment-32, 72, 96, 158
Abuse-96, 158
Actions-156
Addiction-224
Advice1-46
Afraid-22, 36
Age-40, 204
Aloneness-158
Anger-124
Anxiety-86, 98, 116, 132, 152, 176, 224, 250
Ashamed-96
Assumptions-228, 234
Attacked-96
Attachment-58
Attitude-52, 206

Behavior-192
Bemoaning-168
Betrayal-14
Bitterness-174, 234
Brokenness-104, 206
Burdens-82, 176
Busyness-80, 90

Calamity-98, 204, 246
Calm-56, 116
Challenge-70, 102
Chaos-250
Circumstances-78
Clutter-116
Complaints-166, 174, 200
Confusion-34, 116, 120
Correction-212, 242
Courage-144
Crises-56, 64, 122

Danger-98, 246
Darkness-186
Death-152, 246
Deception-62
Decisions-116, 226
Defenseless-12
Dependent-176
Depression-104, 106, 118, 154
Despair-30, 36, 106
Despondency-90
Difficulties-46, 78, 92, 148, 150, 158

Directionless-20
Disappointment-66, 96
Disbelief-200
Discomfort-58
Discontentment-174, 204
Discouragement-24, 36, 72, 106, 126, 144, 248
Discrimination-158
Disheartened-134
Disposition-78
Distractions-80, 82, 162
Doubt-38, 60, 88, 144, 156, 160, 178, 196, 202, 244, 248, 250
Downcast-180
Dread-186

Emptiness-66, 134
Enslaved-234
Evildoers-114

Failure-50, 60
Falsehoods-94
Fear-56, 62, 70, 72, 74, 102, 108, 112, 122, 130, 138, 152, 154,

156, 158, 170, 172, 178, 182, 186, 190, 200, 206, 218, 222
Finances-114, 224, 248, 250, 252
Forebodings-132, 240
Forgiveness-158
Frustration-114, 124, 166
Future-208

Giving up-110, 142
Grief-16, 120

Hardship-142, 204
Heartache-204
Helplessness-150, 158, 182
Hesitation-202, 248
Hiding-96, 98
Haplessness-150
Hopelessness-16, 44, 126, 132, 150, 160, 234

Ignored-96
Impatience-42, 110, 242
Imperfection-210
Impossibilities-48
Illness-76, 156, 164
Inadequacy-70
Insignificant-136

Jealousy-92, 174

Lack-112, 130, 144, 184, 224, 248

Lackluster-132
Lies-154
Limits-208
Listening-220
Loneliness-156, 206
Loss-94, 148
Lost-10, 76
Lowly-136

Marriage-78
Materialism-58
Memories-58
Misaligned-162
Misperception-70
Missteps (Sins)-156
Money matters-76, 114, 130, 140, 240
Motives-238
Muddled-164, 176, 206

Needs-224
Negative attitude/thoughts-54, 104, 110, 156, 160, 168, 216, 226, 232, 234, 236, 240, 244
Neglected-10

Obstacle-70, 102, 178
Oppression-158
Overlooked-10
Overwhelm-128

Pain-208

Panic-98, 158, 170, 186, 228
Passionless-134
Past-58, 208, 234
Perspective-202, 240
Plans-50, 52, 62
Possessions-58, 140, 224
Power-222
Powerless-8, 22, 136, 148, 234
Prayers unanswered-90
Preconceived ideas-84
Pride-84, 198, 216
Priorities-162
Problems-94, 176, 246
Protection-230
Provision-230

Rebuffed-96
Refused-96
Rejection-148
Relationships-248
Reputation-210
Revenge-148

Self-confidence-216
Self-pity-118
Self-willed-194
Sexism-24
Shaken-138
Sleep-190
Sore-76
Sorrow-150
State of mind-204
Strength-28

Stress-86, 118, 164

Strife-188

Stuck (mentally, emotionally, spiritually)-180

Suffering-120, 246

Temptation-58, 140

Tired-76, 118, 126, 164

Tough times-52

Trapped-200

Trouble/Troubled-22, 56, 68, 120, 148, 156, 194, 200, 204, 208, 234, 248

Trust-56, 160, 246, 252

Uncertainty-16, 20, 28, 38, 116, 146, 160, 186, 214

Uncomfortable-60

Unconfident-26, 28

Unexpected-100

Unfulfilled-44

Unhappiness-90, 204

Unkindness-114

Unloved-18, 206

Unnoticed-10

Unpreparedness-58

Unprotected-12

Unworthiness-112

Upset-80

Victim mentality-52

Wandering-162

Weakness-16, 72, 92, 122, 158, 176, 204

Weeping-120, 176

What-ifs-60, 64, 86, 112, 116, 190

Words-74, 156

Work-168, 240, 244

Worn-142

World (ways and customs)-192

Worry-26, 80, 86, 94, 122, 130, 152, 156, 176, 186, 190, 222, 224, 252

Worst-case scenario-64

Worthiness (not good enough)-14